T0166062

PREACHING TO HISPANIC IMMIGRANTS

PRACTICAL ADVICE FOR EFFECTIVENESS

Dr. Pablo J. Rivera Madera

Order this book online at www.trafford.com
or email orders@trafford.com

Most Trafford titles are also available at major online book retailers.

Printed in the United States of America.

ISBN: 978-1-4669-0002-8 (sc)

Trafford rev. 10/10/2011

www.trafford.com

North America & international
toll-free: 1 888 232 4444 (USA & Canada)
phone: 250 383 6864 ♦ fax: 812 355 4082

CONTENTS

Preface...ix

Abstract...xi

Dedication and Aknowledgement xiii

Chapter 1: Hispanic Immigrants in the United States and
    Preaching 2
        Demography and Religious Behavior.............................6
        The Hispanic Community in the United States................7
        The Hispanic Community and Religion 12
        Immigration and the Church 14
        Preaching and the Hispanic Community......................15
        Goals of the Sermon...18
        Models of Preaching...20
        Biblical Model of Preaching..21
        Rhetorical Model of Preaching 24
        Relational Model of Preaching.....................................28
        Preaching for the Latino Community...........................32
        Basic Structure of the Research...................................33

Chapter 2: Methodology 35
        Research Design 35
        Study Variables..36
        Dependent Variable..36
        Independent Variable 36
        Research Questions 37
        Hypotheses...37
        Unit of Analysis...38
        Inclusion Criterion...38

Instrument for Data Collection Collect the Data 38
Pilot Testing 39
Data Collection Procedure 39
Sampling Design 40
Data Analysis Procedure 41
Operational Definition of Concepts 42

Chapter 3: Findings and Analysis 46
Country of Origin, Gender and Age......................................46
Denomination...46
Education...47
Development of Preaching Ministries...................................48
Frequency of Preaching and Language Used 49
Goals of Preaching 50
The Dominant Preaching Model for
      Hispanic Immigrants..51
Rhetorical Model of Preaching 53
The Relational Model of Preaching 55
Opinion of Their Own Model of Preaching 56
Styles of Preaching in Congregations of
      Hispanic Immigrants..57
Preparation and Construction of the Sermon 57
The Use of the Lectionary and the Bible 58
Delivery of the Sermon 58
Reception of the Sermon by the Congregation 60
Main Concerns of Preachers in Hispanic Congregations 62

Chapter 4: Conclusions, Limitations and Recommendations 66
Conclusions 66
Profile of a Hispanic Preacher..68
Goal of Preaching of Hispanic Clergies 68
Model of Preaching 68
Styles of Preaching...69
Structure of the Sermon 70
Delivery of the Sermon 71
Reception of the Message 72
Limitations..73
Recommendations...73

Recommendations from Hispanic Preachers.........................74
Recommendations for Non-Hispanic Clergies
    from the Research...77

Appendices...79
    Letter of Introduction in English............................80
    QUESTIONNAIRE..80
    Letter of Introduction in Spanish 86
    CUESTIONARIO..86

Selected Bibliography 95

LIST OF TABLES

Table 1. Denominational Distribution by Ethnicity 6

Table 2. Religious Tradition among Hispanics,
   by Education among Hispanics 9

Table 3. Frequency of Participants by Denomination 47

Table 4. Geographical Location of Ministry 48

Table 5. Goals of Preaching in Hispanic Congregations...................50

Table 6. Values for the Use of the Biblical Model of Preaching 52

Table 7. Values for the Use of the Rhetorical
   Model of Preaching 53

Table 8. Values for the Relational Model 55

Table 9 Physical Response as a Sign of Approval............................60

Table 10. Verbal Signs of Effectiveness for a Sermon.......................61

Table 11. Emotional Sign of Effectiveness of the Sermon 61

Table 12. Main Concern of Hispanic Preachers 63

PREFACE

Preaching To Hispanic Immigrants: Practical Advice For Effectiveness

This book is in response to the concern of many non-Hispanic religious leaders and churches on how to reach out to the Hispanic community through an effective preaching. Their interest for a pertinent and respectful proclamation to this large segment of the population prompted the questions about models and styles of preaching. Hispanics are growing in the United States and the church in the mainland cannot close its eyes to this reality. In order to give non-Hispanic clergies empirical answers the author conducted a research to provide non-Hispanic clergies with a response grounded in the experience of Hispanic preachers serving in the United States. My intent is to offer non-Hispanic religious leaders knowledge based on the experience of others. The aspiration of non-Hispanic clergies to reach out to the Hispanic group in this country is evidence that the church as a community of faith can bring together people of all nationalities using the proclamation of the Word as its primary means of connection. Hispanics have suffered the alienation from the church in the mainland due to language barrier and cultural background. The gospel is a vehicle of healing and unity with the power to promote the healthy integration of Hispanics to their new environment. Preaching can bring communities together. This book will give non-Hispanic leaders general knowledge and skills to craft and deliver their sermons with sensibility and connection. The findings of this study and the recommendations offered in this book to non-Hispanics pastors have been validated by relevant literature about the subject of preaching.

This book will help non-Hispanic preachers to connect with Latinos with a relevant, interesting and passionate message. Non Hispanic clergies will meet the challenge to proclaim the truth of the gospel in such a way that will cause Hispanics to listen and respond to the gospel of our Lord Jesus Christ.

ABSTRACT

The Dominant Model and Style Of Preaching For Hispanic Immigrants: Practical Advice For Effectivenesss

The book presents the dominant model and style of preaching for congregations with Hispanic immigrants in the United States. The purpose of this research was to support non-Hispanic religious leaders in their efforts to reach out to the Hispanic community.

In this book the author presents three models of preaching and concluded that the biblical model of preaching is the most dominant approach of proclamation in Hispanics congregations. However, this model of preaching does not exclude the others two selected models, the rhetorical and the relational. Also, the study revealed that the style of preaching in the Hispanic setting is participatory because the congregation has an active role during preaching. This book offers guidelines to non-Hispanic religious leaders based on the experience of Hispanic preachers of different educational level on how to reach out to the Hispanic community.

The research sustained that not all the preachers in the Hispanic church possess formal theological education. They function as ordained ministers or lay leaders. Also, a college degree is not essential for the development of the preacher role in the Latino setting. The average length of active ministry is fourteen years. The research explored about the main goal of preaching in the Hispanic religious setting and revealed that the evangelistic purpose drives clergies when address the Latino immigrants through preaching.

DEDICATION AND AKNOWLEDGEMENT

This publication is dedicated to my Redeemer and Savior, Jesus Christ. He transformed my goals in life and taught me that everything is possible with Him. God gave me the awareness of the importance of education to better serve His people. This book is a testimony of the endurance that comes from God. This accomplishment is also dedicated to my parents Pablo Rivera Villegas and Maria Madera Jimenez. They taught me the value of hard work and perseverance.

My family has been a source of strength and affirmation during the long days it took for me to complete this project. Each one of them became an inspiration to fulfill my goal. I dedicate this dissertation to them. They serve God and work for the improvement of the quality of life of His children. This dissertation is dedicated to them for being a blessing in my in life and in my ministry to God. They are a source of energy and inspiration to me, making of my journey a significant experience.

This book is the outcome of God's guidance and intervention in my life. The honor and the glory belong to God. This accomplishment evidences the efforts of many people who supported my vision. Their opinion and assistance contributed to complete this project. Thanks to all the ministers and lay preachers that answered the questionnaires and helped me to reach out to a larger representative sampling. Thanks to those who advised me and gave their candid suggestions for the success of this project. Thanks to all who provided pertinent literature that expanded my knowledge about the subjects included in this research. God bless you. A special gratitude is extended to my editor Mercedes

García Colón. Her commitment and dedication were essential for the success of this project.

My sincere thank you is extended to Mrs. Mae Ann White who made corrections to the multiple drafts and helped me to produce a better document. I am grateful to God for the advice and support of my son, Pablo Rene, who supervised the methodology process for this investigation. He was always present and made me feel on safe ground when I thought I was lost in the process. To all of them a heartfelt thanks!

My acknowledgements to my family for the support and care I received from each of them for the completion of this task. My family was always willing to listen to my ideas, concerns and frustrations and showed constantly the real meaning of love. I count my family as a precious blessing from my Creator.

CHAPTER 1

Hispanic Immigrants in the United States and Preaching

CHAPTER 1

Hispanic Immigrants in the United States and Preaching

Immigration of Hispanics is one of the most important issues in the United States. The Hispanic community has become the largest and fastest growing minority group.[1] The fact that most Hispanics are Christians[2] represents an enormous challenge to the Christian churches in the mainland. The successful interaction among the religious groups in the United States and the Hispanic community demands an intentional ministry and a well defined preaching approach.

The transforming force of the Hispanic community is producing major changes in the American society and in its religious environment. The number of Hispanics increased fifty-eight percent since 1990. It is estimated that 35.3 million Hispanics live in the United States representing over twelve percent of the population of this country.[3]

The social and emotional factors of Hispanic immigrants, along with their process of acculturation, contribute to the complexity of the religious challenge. Although the Spanish language constitutes the primary common factor, Hispanics vary in terms of religion, race,

---

[1] Edwin I. Hernandez et al., *Strengthening Hispanic Ministry across Denominations: A Call to Action* (Durham: Duke Divinity School, 2005), 26.

[2] Ibid., 7.

[3] U.S. Department of Commerce, Census Bureau (Washington, D.C.: U.S. Government Printing Office), 2000.

national origin, ancestral homeland, cultural heritage and memories of a shared historical past.

The classification by the United States Immigration and Naturalization Service of Hispanic immigrants adds to the issue of the diversity among Latinos in this country. This distinction includes immigrants that arrive with investment capital or high educational credentials versus the immigrants who have only their labor to sell.[4] Some immigrants arrive legally and receive assistance from the government for their relocation while still others are categorized as illegal and face legal consequences. Illegal immigration is based on three categories: illegal entry, visa overstay, and the violation of terms.[5]

The data collected by the Current Population Survey (CPS) from March through January 2006 revealed that the illegal immigrant population in the United States is about 12 million people. Pew Hispanic Center has estimated that fifty seven percent (57%) of illegal immigrants come from Mexico; twenty four percent (24%) from Latin America and nineteen percent (19%) from elsewhere.[6] As of 2005, there were 6.6 million families in which either the head of the family or the spouse was an illegal immigrant. These unauthorized families comprise 14.6 million persons. Nearly two-thirds (64%) of the children living in illegal immigrant families are U.S. citizens by birth, an estimated 3.1 million children in 2005.[7]

In the past few years, only persons granted refugee status or legally admitted received any form of official assistance. Since 1996 most immigrants are admitted into the country without government benefits and have been excluded from welfare programs, Medicaid and supplemental security income.[8]

Immigrants are in a much inferior economic situation when compared to the native born Americans. The poverty rate among the

---

[4]   Ibid., 20.

[5]   Ibid., 22.

[6]   Jeffrey S. Passel, The Size and Characteristics of the Unauthorized Migrant Population in the U.S. Estimates Based on the March 2005 Research Report Current Population Survey, (Research Report), The Pew Hispanic Center, March 7, 2006 available from http://pewhispanic.org/files/reports/61.pdf; Internet.

[7]   Ibid.

[8]   Portes, 20.

United States native born Americans in 2002 was more than eleven percent (11.1%), but among Mexican immigrants it reached over twenty four percent (24.4 %), and among Dominicans, over twenty five percent (25.8%).[9] Over twelve percent (12.2%) of the native born Americans did not have health insurance. However, of the Hispanics immigrants who also lacked health care coverage, 53.4% were Mexican, 53.7% were Salvadoran, and 55.8% were Guatemalan.[10]

The socioeconomic status of these immigrants challenges the government and the Church because this sector of the population receives low wages, lives below the poverty line, and many of them do not have health insurance.[11]

The Latino community is in the United States to stay. If immigration continues at current levels, the nation's population will increase from 301 million today to 468 million in 2060, a 167 million (56 percent) increase. Immigrants plus their descendents will account for 105 million (63 percent) of the increase. The above projection follows exactly the Census Bureau's assumptions about future birth and death rates, including a decline in the birth rate for Hispanics, who comprise the largest share of immigrants.[12]

The rapid increase of Hispanics in the United States, their varied social conditions, and the diversity of their religious expressions represent a new phenomenon that confronts Christian churches in this country. This segment of the population brings with them cultural issues of identity that affect their religious integration in a new urban setting. The particularity of the culture challenges the social, economic, political and spiritual environments of the Hispanic community.[13] The idiosyncrasies of this growing segment of the population are transforming the nation's religious composition and

---

[9] Ibid.,24.

[10] Ibid.

[11] Ibid.

[12] Steven A. Camarota, 100 Million More Projecting the Impact of Immigration On the U.S. Population, 2007 to 2060, Center for Immigration Studies *Backgrounder,* August 2007; available from http://www.cis.org/articles/2007/back707.html

[13] David A. Badillo, introduction to *Latinos in the Immigrant Church* (Baltimore: The John Hopkins University Press., 2006), xxvi.

thus, the performance of ministry across the nation.[14] According to Edwin Hernandez, researcher at Notre Dame's Center for the Study of Latino Religion, the Church is the place to transmit, enhance and preserve cultural values. The involvement and active participation of Hispanics in the Church facilitate the transmission of cultural values into the public life.[15]

The understanding of the religious faith of Hispanics is essential for a worship experience that integrates diverse culture and spiritual conviction. Clergies and religious leaders must be aware of the particularity of this community and their religious background in order to be effective in reaching out to them. The unique reality of Hispanics demands accuracy and a sense of purpose in preaching as an act of ministry. Preaching as an instrument for spiritual transformation and social development must be intentional especially as it is meant to be relevant to the Hispanic context.

The National Summit of Hispanic Religious Leaders, held at Duke University in October 2003, concluded that churches must see the Latino presence and the growing of this ethnic group in the United States as a challenge in terms of the cultural multiplicity of the nation. The survivability of the Church as agent of mission depends on its capacity to move across the various cultural groups.[16]

The experience of Hispanic clergies preaching to Latino immigrants could be helpful for the Church in the United States to meet the challenge. The insight and opinion of Hispanic clergies about their most effective paradigm on preaching could help non-Hispanic clergies to fulfill the spiritual needs of this significant group of Christians.

---

[14] Patricia Fernandez Kelly and William Haller, "Religion the Enduring Presence" in *A Portrait Immigrant America,* 3d ed (Berkeley and Los Angeles: University of California Press, 2006), 306-310.

[15] Kim Lawton, "Immigration Fuels Hispanic Church Activity Latino Evangelicals have been Voting Republican, but may be Shifting", Religion & Ethics News Weekly, 11 February 2006, 7.

[16] Hernandez, 12.

Demography and Religious Behavior

Hispanics are profoundly religious and their congregations are growing around the country. This development transcends denominational boundaries involving Catholics and Protestants.[17] The religious beliefs and affiliation of Hispanics represent a continuation of the cultural tradition learned and brought from the home country or an emergent product created by the realities of the new country. Hispanic immigrants and their children generally stay with the religious preference of their families.[18]

Research by the Pew Hispanic Center and the Pew Forum on Religion and Public Life revealed the complexity of the religious behavior of Hispanics. The study was conducted from August 10 to October 4 in 2006 and comprised a sample of 4,016 national Latino respondents. Table 1 presents the results of the survey.

Table 1. Denominational Distribution by Ethnicity

Denomination	Hispanics	Caucasian	African American
Catholic	67.6	22.4	4.2
Protestant	19.6	57.1	82.9
Pentecostal	6.9	3.2	10.3
Baptist	0.1	16.7	46.2
Church of Christ	0.7	2.2	3.1
Presbyterian	0.3	3.4	2.8
Methodist	0.3	9.2	5.4
Lutheran	0.2	6.3	0
Episcopalian	0.2	1.7	0.4
Reformed	0	0.6	0

---

[17] Justo L. Gonzalez and Pablo A. Jimenez, *Pulpito: An Introduction for Hispanic Preaching* (Nashville: Abingdon Press, 2005), x

[18] Portes, 325.

Nondenominational	36.2	6.1	
Something else	2.3	3.8	5.4
Nothing in particular	1.5	3.7	3.2

Source: Report on Pew Forum and Public Life; U.S. Religion Survey (Pew Research Center for the People and Press), July 2006, 8.

The findings reflected that more than eighty-eight percent (88%) of Hispanics are Christians. Sixty-eight percent (68.0%) are Roman Catholics. Protestants constitute twenty percent (20%).[19] The percentages in Table 1 compare the distribution of Christians among different denominations of Christian churches in the United States by ethnicity. The data above reflect that by the year 2006 over two-thirds of Hispanics were Catholics.[20]

The religious behavior of Hispanic Christians is directly related to the unique relationship of Latinos to the Catholic Church and to the religious syncretism in their respective countries. Many Hispanics join the Protestant church but keep their Catholic religious beliefs and behavior.[21] However, the good relationship among Catholics and Protestants allows them to work together on behalf of the Latino community embracing common causes such immigration reform as their moral imperative. The religious tradition of the Hispanic community is a powerful force that expresses a strong sense of identity and preserves customs and language.

The Hispanic Community in the United States

The Hispanic community as the largest minority group in the United States increased from 7.9 percent in 1990 to over 12 percent (12.5%) in 2005. By the year 2020 this sector of the population will be approximately 52.7 million and by the year 2040 Latinos will be about

---

[19] Gregory A. Smith, *Report on Pew Forum and Public Life; U.S. Religion Survey* (Pew Research Center for the People and Press, July 2006), 6.

[20] Ibid.

[21] Badillo, 185.

80.2 million. In 2050 Hispanics will constitute over 24.5% of the U.S. population with 96.5 million.[22]

Hispanics are a highly heterogeneous population. Even the term "Hispanic" is controversial since it does not indicate the influence of the indigenous cultures. Hispanics share common characteristics, such as background of Spanish language and some customs and traditions, like the celebration of the Three Kings Day and the solemnity of the Holy Week. However, there are distinct differences between and within the different groups of Latinos.[23] In physical characteristics, the appearance of Hispanics varies greatly, including resemblance to North American Indians, Blacks, and Europeans. As a group, Hispanics in the United States are a very young population with an average age almost ten years younger than White Americans and two years younger than Black Americans.[24]

Hispanics in the United States are situated in metropolitan areas and populate every state, including Alaska and Hawaii. Some individuals are more oriented toward their particular ethnic group, while others are quite acculturated to mainstream values. Some have lived for generations within the United States, even while the country has experienced a constant flow of recent immigrants.[25]

One of the reasons for the increase of Hispanics in the United States is the implementation of the Immigration and Nationality Act of 1965. This Act abolished the immigration quota system effective since 1920 and facilitated the entrance for family members of legal residents.[26]

The urban presence of Hispanics, beyond Mexican American, Puerto Ricans and Cubans, has been raised by constant immigration. Most of the Hispanic immigrants that benefited from the Act of 1965

---

[22] Ibid., 16.

[23] Derald Wing Sue and David Sue, *Counseling the Culturally Different, Theory and Practice.* 2d ed (Toronto: John Wiley and Sons, 1990), 227.

[24] P. Odin, "Hispanics Help Shape the Educational Landscape. Black Issues in Higher Education" (1987) quoted in Derald Wing Sue, *Counseling the Culturally Different*, 228.

[25] K.A. Moore, "Time to take a Closer Look at Hispanic Children and Families," *Policy and Public Human Services*, 59, 8.

[26] Portes, 12.

arrived from Guatemala, the Dominican Republic, Colombia and other countries from South and Central America.[27]

Latino immigrants have a variety of professional and social levels. According to the Bureau of Census fifty seven percent (57.0%) of Hispanics have a high school diploma while only eleven percent of Latinos (11.1%) have a college degree.

Table 2. Religious Tradition among Hispanics,
by Education among Hispanics

	Hispanics	Catholic	Evangelical	Protestant	Christian	Secular
Education						
Less than high school	39	42	34	30	37	33
High school degree	47	44	54	56	52	49
Four years college	10	9	10	12	9	

Source: Report on Pew Forum and Public Life; U.S. Religion Survey (Pew Research Center for the People and Press), July 2006, 8.

The unemployment rate among Hispanics in May 2009, over twelve percent, (12.2%), is higher than the rate of unemployed Americans (8.6 percent). According to the Bureau of Labor Statistics, Hispanics have had the largest increase in unemployment since the start of the recession in the country.[28] Some Hispanics are blue collar workers and hold semi-skilled occupations in the service industries. Most of them accept jobs in agriculture, gardening, construction work, and nannying.[29]

---

[27] Badillo,182.

[28] U.S. Department of Labor, Bureau of Labor Statistic (Washington, D.C.: Government Printing Office), May 2009.

[29] González, 49.

Poverty among Hispanics is high. Nearly forty percent (40%) of Hispanic children live in poverty compared to thirteen percent (13.2%) of White children. Most Hispanics, especially recent immigrants, live in sub-standard housing.[30]

There is a significant discrepancy between the annual income of Hispanics and native born Americans. Also, Hispanics have disproportionately high rates of tuberculosis, AIDS, and obesity. Nearly forty percent (40%) of men and forty-eight percent (48%) of women are overweight, which increases the risk for developing diabetes and other negative medical conditions. Among Hispanic farm workers, infant mortality rates are as high as twenty five percent (25%). This group is fifty times more likely than the general population to have parasitic infections.[31] The health problem among Hispanics is aggravated by the fact that thirty percent (30%) of Hispanic children are not covered by health insurance as compared to four percent (4%) of Whites and twenty percent (20%) of African Americans.[32]

As Justo L. Gonzalez suggests in his book *Púlpito*, Hispanics are aware that their social boundaries affect adversely their aspirations to transcend their social reality. This community constantly confronts prejudice and a harmful image that displays them as drug addicts, drug dealers, criminals, prostitutes or welfare recipients. This negative picture hinders the opportunities of the Latino to succeed and preserves the wrong idea that Hispanics are morally corrupt and intellectually inferior.[33]

The marginalization and perception of inferiority create a sense of inequality that limits the participation of Hispanics in the centers of decisions related to politics, economics and education. This social dynamic contributes to their lack of power and their acceptance of social boundaries as normal.[34]

Hispanics have a strong emphasis on large families. Fifty-four percent (54%) of Hispanic households are composed of four or more people, compared to twenty-eight percent (28%) for the country as

---

[30]   Sue, 228.

[31]   Ibid.

[32]   Portes, 131.

[33]   Gonzalez, 52.

[34]   Portes, 132.

a whole.[35] Family tradition, unity, respect and loyalty to the family are significant values. This group encourages cooperation rather than competition among family members. The large network of family and friends functions as a stable support system and nurtures their interpersonal relationships.[36]

The extended family includes not only the relatives but often non-blood "relatives" such as best man, maid of honor, and godparents. Each member of the family has a role: grandparents are a source of wisdom and resourcefulness. The mother is identified by her abnegation to the family and the father is the provider. The role of the children is to obey their parents and adults.[37] Most Hispanics keep an emotional involvement and continue obligations with a large number of family and friends in their country of origin and in the U.S. This relationship may become a source of stress because the allegiance to the family is of primary importance, and it takes precedence over any outside concerns, such as attendance at school, church or work.

The issue of the generational gap is another source of tension among Hispanics because this group lives in a country of distinctive values. Some members of this community maintain their traditional orientation, whereas others assimilate easier the American values. The new generations are reluctant to behave and to speak differently than their peers from the dominant U.S. culture. The complexity of the reaction of the second generation may include dissatisfaction with the religion of their parents, family conflicts, and disappointment with their parents.[38]

In their attempt to move away from their traditions, the newer generations explore other alternatives to fulfill their emotional and spiritual needs. The free "market place" for religion offered by American society provides these young people with the opportunity to search for alternatives other than those learned at home.[39] This conflictive relationship among members of Hispanic families affects their interaction within the American society including the Church.

---

[35] Sue, 344.

[36] Ibid., 346.

[37] Ibid.

[38] Portes, 327.

[39] Ibid.

Culture is another central issue for Hispanic immigrants in the United States. The language is the same, but the inflections and some words are different. Also, the social customs among Hispanics reflect their country of origin. These differences provoke conflict and competition among the varying Hispanic groups because of their pride for their respective culture of origin.[40] Clergies must be aware of the dynamic of this issue because it could hinder the cohesion and sense of belonging among the different groups of Hispanics that attend the church.

Latino culture in the United States is evolving into something different from any of the cultures of Latin America. The Hispanic culture in the United States exists within the context of another culture that holds the centers of power, communication and education. Preaching to Hispanics requires a clear understanding of the social dynamics that this segment of the population confronts daily. These social forces influence the self image, cohesion and integration of Hispanics as a community and emphasize the role of religion in the process of adaptation.

The Hispanic Community and Religion

The immigration of Hispanics to the United States is challenging the Christian Church in the mainland and is promoting a new religious behavior. The syncretism of Catholic elements in the Protestant setting makes the religious behavior of this group particular. The religious impact of Hispanic immigrants to mainland churches is greater than the impact caused to the American church by the Irish and German immigration.[41]

A historical study, conducted by Joy Dolan, of the old immigrant church in the United States with emphasis on Irish Americans and German Americans in New York concluded that the Catholicism brought from Europe in the nineteenth century was a religion formed in great part by the Council of Trent without a solid penetration among the grassroots. The attendance at Sunday Mass and the reception of

---

[40]   Gonzalez, 28.

[41]   Badillo, 184.

the Sacraments served as indicators of the religious commitment for Irish and German immigrants. The European church in the nineteenth century was urban, white, and middle class[42] while the Hispanic church is mostly a suburban and lower class church.

Most Hispanics believe that their local patron saints have power to perform miracles against plagues, droughts and other disasters. [43] According to the theologian Anthony Steven Arroyo, the root of the Hispanic religion is directly related to the Catholic Church and to rosaries, passion plays, and devotional prayers in an artistic style that appeals to the emotions.[44]

The centrality of symbols and rituals provides a sense of community to Hispanics living in United States. The theologian Allan Figueroa Deck considers that the ancient pre-modern roots of Latin American cultures remain quite vital in contemporary religious behavior and provide Hispanics with a sense of being a people, and a community.[45] This ethnic group retains a religious emphasis on family, children, and immediate community. They live a traditional, nostalgic and conservative faith in order to preserve and transmit their identity and culture. They are more conservative in the United States than in their native country in the expression of their popular religion.[46]

Sociologist Stephen Warner found that the religious pluralism has led to the reinforcement of identity for new immigrants. Latinos effectively use religion as a vehicle for recreating identities, stabilizing families and adapting to neighborhoods especially while facing socioeconomic crisis and urban anomie.[47] The Church has always developed an active role for the transmission of identity across generations. Sociologists Anna Peterson, Manuel Vasquez, and Phillip Williams describe the Church with the power to ease dislocation and fragmentation in a changing context. In their view, Christianity expands traditional roles, questions

---

[42] Ibid.

[43] Ibid., 185.

[44] Ibid., 186.

[45] Ibid., 187.

[46] Ibid., 191.

[47] Ibid., 192.

traditional boundaries and emphasizes Sacraments and spiritual renewal.[48]

In the particular case of Hispanic immigrants, they have merged religion with economic, political and social activities. Religion influences their daily life and is a source of comfort in times of stress. Hispanics strongly believe in prayer and in active participation in religious events. Most of them believe that a sacrifice in this world is helpful to salvation and that promoting charity to others is one of the most important virtues.[49] Hispanics often feel resigned to their fate because life's misfortune is seen as inevitable. Many of them believe that some spirits can cause mental and physical health problems and this belief affects their assertiveness.[50]

Immigration and the Church

The immigrants attending congregations in the United States have common issues. They need work, shelter, interpersonal connections, and orientation about government services, physical care, emotional adjustment, and spiritual guidance. Many of them confront difficulty adapting to the pressure of this country because they do not know English as a second language. Hispanic immigrants experience lack of public services and, in some cases, exploitation by employers, and lack of opportunities for them and their families.[51]

Some Hispanic immigrants have a constant apprehension of the possible loss of their underpaid employment and bring this fear to the Church. If they are in this country illegally, they face fear of being deported. Most of them are reluctant to provide private information or to make long-term commitments. They also bring to the Church the emotional aspects of their relationship with their family. The ties to their families in their countries have a direct impact on their economic,

---

[48]   Ibid.

[49]   Sue, 351.

[50]   Ibid.

[51]   Justo L. Gonzalez, *Mañana: Christian Theology from a Hispanic Perspective* (Nashville: Abingdon Press, 1990), 35.

social, and political views and affect the way they approach religion.[52] Their loyalty to the country of their ancestors provokes daily feelings of separation, isolation and loneliness. This experience is more difficult if the immigrants are in the country illegally and cannot go back to their country of origin without facing legal consequences.

Preaching and the Hispanic Community

The issue of the Hispanic immigration has a direct impact on the Church and how its clergy preach. Hispanic congregations conceive preaching as a communal act.[53] In worship, they integrate their daily experiences and expect a direct connection with the preachers through the sermon. The act of preaching is an encounter between the people and the preacher and cannot be reduced to a manuscript.[54]

The Hispanic worship environment demands the interaction between the preacher and the congregation. David Kenneth Davis in his book, *Preaching and Culture in Latino Congregations*, states that the task to preach effectively to people living in the situation of many Hispanics is not easy. A typical congregation will have a mixture of Hispanics from various countries, diverse levels of acculturation and particular histories of suffering.[55]

The act of preaching in this setting is participative and personal. Preachers in this setting must have credibility and connection. Credibility is based on their religious background, credentials and personal testimony of the preachers. Connection is possible when the congregation perceive that preachers share the same cultural values. The lack of connection interferes with the best receptivity of the message and adversely affects the response of some Hispanics congregations to the preaching experience. Preachers in this environment must understand the experience of suffering and struggles of this particular group.[56]

---

[52] Ibid., 37.

[53] Ibid., 59.

[54] Ibid.

[55] Kenneth G. Davis and Jorge L. Presmanes, *Preaching and Culture in Latino Congregations* (Chicago: Training Publications, 2000), 68.

[56] Ibid.

The power of solidarity is essential. Preachers who participate in this solidarity link the class and cultural insights with their proclamation of the Word.[57] The preachers comfort, affirm and challenge the spiritual growth of the people when sharing their own salvation stories through informal conversation.[58]

Hispanic congregations are responsive and provide feedback to let the preachers know that they are receiving the Word. Several manners in which the congregation expresses validation of the message are verbal responses, raising of hands, waving bulletins or handkerchiefs, and other emotional expressions such as tears, sighs, and laughter are normal ways to communicate their fulfillment.[59]

It is important for preachers in this setting to recognize and respond to these signs of connectivity from the people. The interaction between preacher and the audience sometimes creates confusion especially for non-Hispanic preachers. In the Hispanic congregation the manuscript of a sermon and the delivery of a sermon are totally different concepts. They do not see these two elements as part of one unit.[60]

The issue of setting and delivery are integral parts of the sermon and not mere techniques. Preachers must take the setting into account in not only preparing the sermon but also delivering it. The use of language, voice, and gesture are constitutive elements of the sermon. Also, frequency and length are unique characteristics of the setting and practice of preaching in the Hispanic environment.[61]

The preaching of the Word in this setting is frequent, continuous and lengthy. These congregations celebrate three or more services during a week and emphasize preaching in every worship activity. Sermons usually last more than thirty minutes, affecting both structure and preparation. Preachers find difficulty in applying the standard manual of homiletics to sermons of more than twenty minutes. Sermons longer than thirty minutes will have several points and more digressions.[62]

---

[57] Ibid., 73.

[58] Ibid., 71.

[59] Gonzalez, *Pulpito*, 58.

[60] Davis. 48.

[61] Gonzalez, *Pulpito*, 59.

[62] Ibid.,

In order to keep the audience attentive for a longer period, Hispanic preachers tend to be dramatic and to appeal to the emotions.[63] The congregation expects the use of daily experiences and jokes from the pulpit in every sermon as a way of illustration.[64]

Preaching in this context is bicultural because the Church in this environment has various degrees of acculturation. The same congregation represents different generations with the older generation being less acculturated than the younger. The new generation is most adapted to the American culture.[65] The major challenge for preachers in this setting is to effectively deliver a sermon that responds to the expectations, needs, experiences, and perceptions of the various groups within the same congregation.

Wisdom and the Scriptures are important signs of authority. Wisdom as a source of authority combines common sense with personal integrity. It requires vision, sensitivity, seriousness of purpose and even humor.[66] Preachers demonstrate their wisdom by knowing the biblical text, listening to the congregation, and by being in dialogue with the congregation even while preaching. Wisdom is the very essence of a true sermon and Hispanic congregations react to preaching as they would do to an art performance.[67]

The Scriptures are the other source of authority. The content of preaching must be biblically strong. They expect the preacher to build the sermon by threading a series of verses of the Bible, citing chapter and verse. High levels of formal education are not fundamental[68] because education, ordination or appointment as the preacher's source of authority is not essential.

Hispanics approach the Bible as a living word and expect to hear in each preaching something new from the Scriptures. They read the Bible regularly. However, interpretation is subject to their traditional approaches that teach them to read Scriptures in terms of individual religiosity and morality. Preachers should address new situations from

---

[63] Ibid.,60.
[64] Ibid.
[65] Ibid.,61.
[66] Ibid.,64.
[67] Ibid.
[68] Ibid., 65.

the pulpit through the interpretation of the text with authority and freedom.[69]

Hispanic congregations respect the authority of the preacher. The leaders have authority based on their wisdom and ability to connect their preaching with the gospel. Like the role of grandparents or elders in extended families, this authority is given to those leaders whose wisdom has been proven over the years.[70] Davis emphasizes that the theology of preaching for Hispanics is characterized by a theology of the revelation of God in the human experience and the cultural context, the encounter between the tradition of faith and the culture of the local church, the understanding that culture and the history of the congregation enlighten liturgy, and the belief that we can find universal truth in the particularity of the culture.[71]

According to Davis, the cultural context is a privileged source of revelation and preachers must ground their theology of preaching in it.[72] He suggests the need to link the hermeneutical approach of the Bible to the experience of exile of Hispanics. Preaching for the Hispanic community should address hope and grace as its central message. In this context, the reign of God is conceived as a place of hope, rich in diversity and absent of the oppressive contrasting experiences.[73]

Goals of the Sermon

Latino preaching is an act of ministry committed to raise spiritual and social awareness based on the communion and participation of the people. In the preaching, the people are called to embrace and recommit themselves to the service of community.[74] The right approach to preaching in this challenging context will impact the spiritual and social behavior. Preachers have the opportunity to contribute to

---

[69]   Ibid., 18.
[70]   Ibid., 66.
[71]   Davis, 6.
[72]   Ibid., 11.
[73]   Ibid., 15.
[74]   Ibid., 24.

the development of the community of faith through a message that promotes solidarity and hope, especially for the Hispanic immigrants.

Paul Scott Wilson enumerates several goals that can be applied to preaching in any context, but especially in the Hispanic environment. He suggests that the sermon must pursue the following goals, applicable to any model of preaching.[75]

1. Be hopeful.
2. Build up the community of faith.
3. Present the biblical text as the sermon's source.
4. Identify what needs correction in human behavior.
5. Portray human experience in authentic ways.
6. Draw on the rich resources of language, ideas, images, and stories.
7. Guide people to deeper theological awareness.
8. Bring theological reflection to bear on the world.
9. Cast people on God's gracious resources for help.
10. Demonstrate God's action in human affairs.
11. Speak of God in concrete ways as a Person (as one in three persons).
12. Represent tradition faithfully.
13. Proclaim what God has done and is doing.
14. Permit God to speak in present tense unconditional declaration.
15. Empower the individual to greater faith.
16. Equip individuals for lives of faithful service to others.
17. Encourage people to use the gifts God has given them.
18. Promise the resources they will continue to find in God.
19. Point to what God is already doing to change the world.
20. Allow the beginning and the end of time to inform the current time.
21. Attend to sign of trouble and grace as signature of God.
22. Seek echoes of trouble and grace throughout the Bible.
23. Uncover trouble and grace in or behind each biblical text.

---

[75] Paul Scott Wilson, *Preaching and Its Partners: Preaching and Homiletical Theory* (St. Louis, Missouri: Chalice Press, 2004), 99.

24. Preach the Gospel, not just the biblical text.
25. Celebrate the good news.[76]

Models of Preaching

The use of a model of preaching helps preachers to intersect with the world and to be effective in the exposition of the Word. Paul Scott Wilson states that if the Bible does not intersect with our world in an important way in the sermon the whole thing may fall flat.[77] Eugene L. Lowry identifies six models of preaching related to the "new homiletic" voices. He describes in his book, *The Sermon: Dancing the Edge of Mystery*, the following models: the Inductive Sermon, the Story Sermon, the Narrative Sermon, the Transconscious African American Sermon, The Phenomenological Move Sermon and the Conversational-Episodal Sermon.[78]

William E. Hull distinguishes in his book, *Strategy Preaching,* three traditional approaches that have dominated the understanding of preaching. He mentions the biblical model, the rhetorical model, and the relational model.[79]

Paul Scott Wilson emphasizes these models of preaching which identify preaching as an event, preaching as performative word, preaching as transformation, and preaching in terms of language and structure. According to Scott, all these paradigms are, in essence, biblical because preaching is biblical when it is based on the Bible, and when it uses the Bible's words, images, and stories as the basis for what is said. He maintains that the doctrines the church teaches, the

---

[76] The list of characteristics for sermons is the result of consensus within the trouble/grace school of preaching. This school seeks to formulate a way to identify both the divine and human dimensions of texts. These goals are compatible with the preaching in the Hispanic community.

[77] Ibid.,7.

[78] Eugene L. Lowry, *The Sermon: Dancing the Edge of Mystery* (Nashville: Abingdon Press, 1997), 20-28.

[79] William E. Hull, *Strategic Preaching: The Role of the Pulpit in Pastoral Leadership* (St. Louis, Missouri, 2006), 6-12.

sermons it preaches and the social issues the Church embraces all have biblical foundations.[80]

In his *Preaching that Matters*, Stephen Farris addresses the issue in terms of coherence. For this author, preaching may be recognized as the Word of God when it coheres with the biblical witness and the sermon will grow from the interaction of the preacher with a biblical text.[81] Scott sustains this view affirming that good preachers understand that their role is to proclaim God's Word, not their own. God uses the preacher to speak a specific word to a particular congregation that has set apart this person to speak God's Word on their behalf. Preaching can transform people's lives, change the culture, and renew the Church. Preachers can bring hope, healing and light to the community.[82]

There are several approaches in biblical preaching because the Bible, even with all its details, does not make explicit every possible human scenario. This fact creates the necessity to emphasize particular aspects of the biblical text. The selection of a point of emphasis is a small step in the sermon process, but it is the most important step a preacher can make.[83] The distinction among the different paradigms of preaching is relevant because there is not a categorical division line between the different traditional models of preaching.[84]

Biblical Model of Preaching

The book *Bonhoeffer: Worldly Preaching* by Clyde E. Fant makes a distinction between the proclaimed Word from other forms of speech.

---

[80] Ibid.

[81] Stephen Farris, *Preaching That Matters: The Bible and Our Lives* (Louisville: Westminster John Knox Press, 1998), 7, quoted in Paul Scott Wilson, *Preaching and Homiletical Theory* (St. Louise, Missouri: Chalice Press, 2004), 8.

[82] Adam Hamilton, *Unleashing the Word: Preaching With Relevance, Purpose and Passion* (Nashville: Abingdon Press, 2003), 10.

[83] Ibid.

[84] For the purpose of this research we will assess the traditional models of preaching as discussed by William Hull because these emphases integrate a variety approaches to preaching.

Other speeches are structured in some way that they have information not intrinsic to the truth that they want to communicate. The purpose of other speeches is to teach a concept, communicate an idea or express an emotion. In his opinion human words communicate something separate from what they are.[85]

Bonhoeffer stated that the meaning of the proclaimed Word is intrinsic to the Word itself. The objective of the proclaimed Word is to communicate Jesus Christ and this objective distinguishes the preached Word from all other forms of speech. Preaching has the power to transform and sustain the people. Personal agendas or hidden intentions are not part of preaching.

In his book *Conversations with Barth on Preaching*, William H. Willimon discusses the emphasis of the biblical understanding of preaching. He mentions that for Karl Barth, preaching is exposition, not exegesis. It follows the text but moves on from it to the preacher's own heart to the congregation. Preaching is biblical when it is a grateful, joyful, playful submission to and repetition of the biblical text that is a faithful exposition of what God says.[86]

Barth identifies the Word of God in threefold form: the written Word of God, the preached Word of God, and the revealed Word of God. For Barth, preaching rests on a commission that is beyond oneself and must be accepted and received. The Word of God is an event because it is something that God gives fresh, new each day, each moment of revelation.[87] In preaching, Christ comes to us, and the gospel should really not be something written, but a spoken word that God makes known.[88]

Willimon emphasizes that preachers should get themselves out of the way of the Word of God. The goal of preaching is to be transparent to the gospel. Preaching is attesting communication of the biblical message and rests on biblical studies of the declaration and explanation of the gospel. Willimon agrees with the proposition of Karl Barth in

---

[85] Clyde E. Fant, *Bonhoeffer: Worldly Preaching* (Nashville, Tennessee: Thomas Nelson Inc. Publishers, 1975), 128.

[86] William H. Willimon, *Conversations with Barth on Preaching* (Nashville: Abingdon Press, 2006), 26.

[87] Ibid.,170.

[88] Ibid.

terms that the proclaimed Word does not belong to the preacher as a subject matter expert. The preacher is only the servant and helper of the Word. In his understanding, the preacher does not bring the Word into the pulpit for his own uses; instead the Word uses the preacher on behalf of the congregation. The power lies within the Word and not in the preacher and nothing can take the place of the direct message of Jesus Christ.[89] According to Dietrich Bonhoeffer, Christ is alive as the Word of the Father in the proclaimed word. Through the Holy Spirit the incarnate Word comes to us from the Scripture in the sermon.[90] The preacher should be assured that Christ enters the congregation through those words which he proclaims from the Scripture.[91] P.T. Forsyth affirmed the relationship of theology to preaching by establishing the theological principle of grace as the substantive core of all preaching.[92] The sermon must integrate preacher, congregation and Scriptures in an experience of faith.[93]

Ilion T. Jones in his book, *Principles and Practice of Preaching: A Comprehensive Study of the Art of Sermon Construction*, points out that a sermon is not a lecture, an essay, a theological dissertation, a discussion of social, political and world affairs, but the saving approach of God to the people. Preaching is not a human event, but it is the revelation of God in Christ. Preachers are partners with God in His redemptive activity.[94] In his book *A Theology of Preaching: The Dynamic of the Gospel,* Richard Lischer affirms that as long as the preacher believes that it is possible to move directly from text to sermon, the sermon will be awash with unassimilated and unordered biblical assertions. He points out that the preacher as theologian must discover how the gospel opens the door to a correct understanding of the whole Bible.

---

[89]   Ibid.,168.

[90]   Dietrich Bonhoeffer, *Worldly Preaching*, ed.Clyde E. Fant (Nashville and New York: Thomas Nelson Inc, 1975), 129.

[91]   Ibid., 130.

[92]   P.T.Forsyth, Positive Preaching and Modern Mind in Richard Lischer, *Theories of Preaching: Selected Readings in the Homiletical Tradition*, (Durham, North Carolina: The Labyrinth press, 1987), 333-337.

[93]   Ibid.

[94]   Ilion T. Jones, *Principles and Practice of Preaching: A Comprehensive Study of the Art of Sermon Construction* (Nashville: Abingdon, 1981), 19.

Preachers execute the text by helping it to speak to a particular time, situation, and people.[95]

Rhetorical Model of Preaching

The rhetorical paradigm conceives the sermon as a religious performance. In this approach, the divine aspect of the sermon is balanced with its persuasive human aspect in which the preacher states a thesis. This rhetorical theory dates back to at least two centuries before Christ. The classical rhetoric is a formula devised by Hermagoras to discover what can be said about something by inventing an argument or thesis.

In rhetoric, the thesis statement is a complete and declarative single sentence that ensures unity in the final speech. It has a simple sentence with one subject that identifies a particular aspect of the message. The rhetorical approach defines preaching as performative and eventful. The term performative indicates that the thesis is the performance of an action.

This rhetorical model highlights content and semantics more than hermeneutics. In *Design for Preaching*, H. Grady Davis expresses that the sermon exhibits organic growth. The sermon is an idea that grows. It has to answer three questions: What am I to talk about? (The idea must be narrow enough to be sharp.) What does this mean? What must be said? (The idea must have in it a force that is expanding.) In this approach, the main idea must be true. It should connect to the realities of the human heart, life, death and human emotions. A sermon is one of the many facets of the gospel of Christ.[96]

Long and Craddock engage the performative dimension of preaching when dealing with the biblical text rhetorically. They are explicit in naming the biblical text as the source of the theme sentence

---

[95] Richard Lisher, *A Theology of Preaching; The Dynamics of the Gospel*, reprinted revised edition (Eugene, Oregon: Wipf and Stock Publishers, 2001), 59-62.

[96] H. Grady Davis, *Design for Preaching* (Philadelphia: Fortress Press, 1958), 44-54, quoted in Paul Scott Wilson, *Preaching and Homiletical Theory* (St. Louis, Missouri: Chalice Press, 2004), 10.

and in relying on rhetoric to establish it.[97] Craddock practices inductive and narrative preaching. He and Long work with two questions "What is the text saying?" (Focus statement) and "What is the text doing?" (Function statement) They think that the sermon should strive to produce in the congregation something of the rhetorical intent of the text.

In other words, the sermon should perform the text's meaning and function. It should have both content and intent. It should be effective and affective. In this paradigm, the personality of the preacher is central for an effective preaching.

The human dimension of preaching is addressed by Charles L. Bartow in his book *God's Human Speech: A practical Theology of Proclamation*. He defines preaching as a theological enterprise that is embodied at any given time in a human voice, body, and person.[98] Bartow sees the preacher as a public person who puts together theology with other considerations, such as the language, vocal and physical gestures, literary theory and rhetoric, aesthetics, vocal technique, articulation, diction and pronunciation. The dilemma that moves the discussion for Bartow is "if God's speech is not human speech, then God will keep silent. Preachers might as well keep silent too". Bartow concludes that preaching is a human performance enterprise and it is not apart from the content.[99]

In his essay "Preaching as a Communicative Act: the Birth of a Performance" in the *Reformed Liturgy and Music*, Dr. Richard Ward supports the concept of preaching as communication that influences the transaction between preachers and their listeners. In his article, the author applies the idea of performance as a concept that integrates not only the preparation but the delivery of the sermon. Performance

---

[97] Fred B. Craddock, *Preaching* (Nashville: Abingdon Press, 1985), quoted in Scott, 11.

[98] Charles L. Bartow, *God's Human Speech: A Practical Theology of Proclamation* (Grand Rapids, Michigan/ Cambridge, U.K.: William B. Eerdmans Publishing Company, 1997), 5.

[99] Richard Ward, "Preaching as a Communicative Act: The Birth of a Performance" *Reformed Liturgy and Music* 30, no.2, 1996.

combines the elements of language, action, and form, with speech, gesture, and embodiment in the event of preaching.[100]

Thomas G. Long in his book, The *Witness of Preaching*, says that preachers do not come into the Church out of the blue, from some exalted place apart, with a secret knowledge concerning deity. He points out that preachers come from the Church itself, from among the laity in the pew; however, what they preach comes from God and not from the people. They communicate what they have learned, received, heard, and seen in Jesus Christ. Preachers bring their own experience and personal background and must be aware of their own efforts and contexts when preaching the Word.[101]

Phillip Brooks in his *Lectures on Preaching* defines preaching as the communication of truth by man to men, having two interrelated and indivisible essential elements, truth and personality. The truth is the most authoritative statement of God's will, communicated through the personality of the preacher.[102] However, if the person speaks to others something that is not true, or if he uses his power of persuasion or of entertainment to make others listen to individual speculations or to do his will or applaud his cleverness, that is not preaching.[103] The concept of personality for Brooks involves the entire being including character, affection, intellect and morality.

In his book, *The Preacher Portrait*, John R. W. Scott points out the importance of the preacher's personality for an effective encounter with the people. Some of the attributes for effective preaching are message, authority, character of the proclamation, necessity of experience of the gospel, nature of the motive to preach, and source of power. Preachers

---

[100]   Ibid.

[101]   Thomas G. Long, *The Witness of Preaching* (Louisville, KY: Westminster/ John Knox Press, 1989), 10.

[102]   Phillips Brooks, *Lectures on Preaching* (New York: E.P. Dutton&Company, 1907),5-26 in Richard Lischer, *Theories of Preaching: Selected Reading in the Homiletical Tradition* (Durham, North Carolina: The Laberinth Press,1987),14-15.

[103]   Ibid.

must show moral qualities such as humility, gentleness and love in order to be effective in their task of preaching.[104]

In an article excerpted from the book *From Pew to Pulpit: A Beginner's Guide to Preaching*, Glifton E Guthrie expresses that preaching always involves the whole person, including the reality of the body, the timbre of voice, the culture in which the person was raised, the language the preacher speaks, the experiences, even the quality of the faith walk of the preacher.[105] According to Guthrie, good preachers are fully in touch with the limits and gifts of their humanity, but their goal is to use those to point to the gospel.

Willard F. Jabusch is extremely conservative on this approach in his book *The Person in the Pulpit: Preaching as Caring*. His argument is that good preaching comes from good people. Preaching is a means of holiness, and it is not peripheral to the identity of the preacher. He adds that if the Christian Church would hope to be blessed with good preaching on Sundays, it must be deeply concerned with the character of its preachers and the quality of their lives on the other days of the week.[106]

In his book *Designing the Sermon: Order and Movement in Preaching*, James Earl Massey describes the preacher as a medium of contact between God and the minds and hearts of the people. He places both preacher and sermon in the same context. Preachers must have a clear understanding that sermons are part of God's Word and that they as preachers are subject to God's purpose and to the life of the Church.[107]

This rhetorical approach sets the sermon in motion because a preacher goes to a biblical text seeking to hear a word for the life of the

---

[104] John R. W. Scott, *The Preacher's Portrait: Some New Testament Word Studies* (Grand Rapids, Michigan: Wm. B. Eerdmans Publishing Company, 1977), 30 passim.

[105] Glifton E. Guthrie, *From Pew to Pulpit: A Beginner's Guide to Preaching* (Nashville: Abingdon Press, 2006).

[106] Willard F. Jabusch, *The Person in the Pulpit: Preaching as Caring* (Nashville: Abingdon, 1981), 92.

[107] James Earl Massey, *Designing the Sermon: Order and Movement in Preaching* (Nashville: Abingdon, 1981), 18-20.

Church. In this model, the preacher chooses from many concerns of the text and moves from the biblical text into the present.

According to Paul Scott, the text communicates many things, including rhetoric argument, feeling and character. Biblical texts contain images and stories, metaphors and symbols, histories and prophecies and dilemmas. Preaching must transcend time and must bring the congregation into the biblical scene by establishing actual identity of the Bible here and now.[108]

Relational Model of Preaching

The relational model transfers the central concern of preaching from the speaker to the hearers, from the pulpit to the pews. The relational paradigm emerged afresh in the second half of the twentieth century as an effort to provide preachers with more freedom in their exposition of the Word and to liberate them from the claims the other two paradigms made for the sermon.[109]

In the second chapter of the book edited by Arthur Van Seters, *Preaching as a Social Act: Theology and Practice,* Justo L. Gonzalez expresses that the meaning of a sermon is determined by the context in which it is preached. The more the context changes the more the meaning of the sermon itself changes. The act of preaching intersects other contexts at various levels such as social class, liturgical setting, economic conditions, personal struggles, racial prejudice, and denominational traditions. The theological understanding of preaching impacts the development and final results of the act of preaching. According to Gonzalez, preaching should address the situation of the hearers and must consider the need of the parish in connection to the world.[110]

---

[108] Wilson, 12.

[109] William E. Hull, *Strategic Preaching, The Role of the Pulpit in Pastoral Leadership* (St. Louis, Missouri: Chalice Press, 2006), 10.

[110] Justo L. Gonzalez and Catherine G. Gonzalez, *The Larger Context* in Arthur Van Seters., ed. *Preaching as a Social Act: Theology and Practice* (Nashville: Abingdon Press, 1988), available in the internet at http://www. religion-online.org/showchapter.asp?title=1084&c=1109

In *The Practical Preacher,* Paul Edwards expresses that the preacher must validate the message with the people. The gospel should be preached as having its application to every context in the life of every Christian. In his words, to abstain from the earthy gospel is to preach a "mutilated gospel."[111]

The preacher must watch, listen, read, and ask. Preachers have the responsibility to help people grow in their Christian principles. The mission of the preacher is to offer the people the inspiration to give their Christian beliefs concrete realization in the social and political spheres as well in their private lives. Edwards believes that the goal of preaching is to offer the people all the knowledge, understanding and guidance in order that they can learn for themselves and wisely choose their own way.

Alan of Lille in *The Art of Preaching* points out that the goal of Christian preaching is formation because it implies a lifelong process. Preaching is an open and public instruction in faith and behavior in which the human and the divine come together forming the hearers. Preaching should be public because it must be delivered openly and for the edification of the people.[112]

The power of preaching from a contextual point of view is discussed by Barbara K. Lundblad in her book, *Transforming the Stone: Preaching Through Resistance to Change.* The author states that sermons need to speak to a variety of specific life situations within the congregation. Attentive listening to people in the parish and the larger community will reveal deep wounds that have never healed and shame that has never been covered over. She emphasizes that the sermon must be written with the faces and voices of the people in mind because it is important to pay attention to spoken and unspoken stories to bring them into the communal space of worship and preaching.[113]

---

[111] Paul, Edwards, *The Practical Preacher: Handy Hints for Hesitant Homilist* (Collegeville, Minnesota: The Liturgical Press, 1994), 33.

[112] Alan of Lille, *The Art of Preaching,* Cistecian Fathers Series, Number 23, Trans. Gilian R. Evans (Kalamazoo: Cistercian Publications, 1981),15-22 in Richard Lischer, *Theories of Preaching,* 9.

[113] Barbara K. Lundblad, *Transforming the Stone: Preaching through Resistance to Change* (Nashville: Abingdon Press, 2001), 30.

Gennifer Benjamin Brooks, assistant professor of Homiletics at Garrett Evangelical Theological Seminary, sees preaching as an act of Christian worship. According to Brooks, in her article "Preaching as a Liturgical Act," preaching as an act of worship involves both divine revelation and human response. To speak of preaching and worship is to force an unnatural separation of a singular event.[114] Preaching is part of the action where the community gathers to celebrate and participate in the dialogue of proclaiming the work of God in the liturgical environment.

The preacher stands among the people and is charged with the task of enabling the congregation to hear and to see the action of God in the world. By addressing the reality of the congregation's situation, the sermon makes God's presence visible and audible to the people. Authentic preaching takes place when Christ reveals Himself in the context of worship.[115]

Preaching is dialogical and contextual. The gathered community is of primary importance for the preacher and for preaching. Brooks understands that preaching must be contextual for the lives of the congregation and must fit in the context of the worship service.[116]

The relational approach conceives the pulpit as a crucial catalyst in helping the church to fulfill its mission in today's world. William E. Hull in his book, *Strategic Preaching: The Role of the Pulpit in Pastoral Leadership,* says that sermons must move the people of God toward the goals defined by the promises of the gospel. Preaching can enhance leadership and leadership can enhance preaching.[117] This concept has a strategic dimension because it implies a direct connection between preaching and the listeners.

Hull clearly developed the concept of strategic preaching in order to answer fundamental questions of the congregation that are relevant to the relational approach. Why are we here? Where are we going? How are we going to get there? What will be required to make this venture? Who will commit to join us for the journey? Where do we

---

[114] Gennifer Benjamin Brooks, *Preaching as a Liturgical Act*, Circuit Rider, Januay/February, 2006, 11-12.

[115] Ibid.

[116] Ibid.

[117] Hull, 116-118.

go from here?[118] This approach to preaching considers the culture of the congregation essential in the process of preaching. Among those who see multiculturalism as a key factor for effective preaching are: Kathy Black, Christina Smith, Lenora Tubbs Tisdale, Joseph R. Jeter Jr., Ronald J. Allen, James R. Nieman and Thomas G. Rogers.[119]

In this relational approach, preachers and people decide where they are going and the sermon contributes to this end. Preaching should give the Church added purpose and direction. The sermon itself takes movement because it is designed to elicit movement from the congregation toward God's given goals. In this relational approach, the term

"transformational preaching" is relevant. Richard A. Jensen, Lucy Rose and David Brown emphasize this concept. This approach is also known as narrative, imaginative, or existential preaching. Rose prefers transformative because it conveys the belief that the sermons should be an experience that transform the worshippers.[120] The term is used to speak of the final results of preaching in which lives are transformed and conformed to the image of Christ.

For Rose, transformational preaching opens a new way of seeing oneself, one's neighbors and the world. For her, it is preaching that de-emphasizes God: instead of developing an encounter with God it emphasizes more the preacher's responsibility in the sermon's becoming an event.[121] The sermon no longer mediates God and knowledge of God through divine self revelation. In transformational views of preaching, the dominant focus shifts to the human side of the encounter. Such preaching addresses ideas, yet it also assists listener's participation.

Preaching is transformative because God uses it for formation: to form listeners as disciples of Christ and to unite them to the community

---

[118] Richard A. Jensen, *Thinking in Story: Preaching in a post-literate Age* (Lima, Ohio: CSS, 1993, 75. Lucy Atkinson Rose, *Sharing the Word: Preaching in the Roundtable Church* (Louisville: Westminster John Knox, 1997), 59. David M. Brown *Transformational Preaching: Theory and Practice* (Lanham, Md: University Press of America, 2003), quoted in Paul Scott, *Preaching*, 66.

[119] Ibid., 128-131.

[120] Ibid.

[121] Ibid., 67.

of faith. The power of the sermon to transform lives still has more to do with God and faith than with how preachers perform. Preaching is transformative because through preaching people relate to God. Individuals are restored to what God intended, and communities are shaped and empowered for discipleship.[122]

Transformation may be something in which preachers can assist, but it is God's activity that is transformative.[123] In the words of W.E. Sangster, "Preaching is a constant agent of the divine power by which the greatest miracle God ever works is wrought and wrought again. God uses it to change lives."[124] The purpose of preaching is to transform the morale of the society into a caring community in the image of Christ.

Preaching for the Latino Community

How do these models of preaching apply to Christian churches with Hispanic immigrants? What type of preaching is the most effective in reaching out to Hispanic immigrants? The application of the most effective paradigm of preaching in the Hispanic environment is essential to fill the spiritual and emotional needs of this significant segment of the population.

The Hispanic community is pluralistic in ethnicity, race and beliefs. Not all the Hispanics have the same cultural background. This complexity presents a challenge for preachers. Preaching should recognize the sovereignty of the nations to control the flow of immigrants, should promote peace among every person, and uphold the dignity of the human being regardless of social or legal status.

Preaching to the Hispanic community living in the United States requires a clear understanding of the cultural, social and political issues of the nation. The articulation of faith in the midst of a discussion in terms of the status of immigrants demands prayer, serious study of the text and constant monitoring of the context.

The Hispanic community expects from preachers a communication that promotes solidarity from the pulpit. Non-Hispanic preachers

---

[122] Ibid.

[123] ibid., 69.

[124] Ibid., 66.

could confront more difficulty to fulfill this type of expectation than Hispanic preachers who probably have undergone the same struggles of the people that are listening.[125] The Hispanic preachers bring to the pulpit their anxieties, worries and personal understanding of the issues of immigration making solidarity a normal process. The preaching experience of Hispanic clergies can provide guidance to non-Hispanic preachers in their effort to be effective in their exposition of the Word to this community.

It is important to develop an intentional paradigm related to the needs of the people in order to be effective in reaching out to this important group of the population in the United States. Preachers are called to understand the suffering and concerns of the people with a clear purpose of bringing clarity, solidarity and hope to the community of faith, including the Hispanic immigrants.

Basic Structure of the Research

This study is a quantitative cross-sectional design to explore the model of preaching that Hispanic clergies use in their interaction in congregation with Hispanic immigrants. Also, this research examines the relationship between model of preaching and style of preaching for Hispanic immigrants that attend to Christian churches in the United States. This study offers guidelines to non-Hispanic clergies based on the experience of Hispanic preachers on how to reach out to the Hispanic community.

It is important to understand the Latino culture and its function in the church, recognizing the strengths that exist in this community and the struggles that this segment of the population faces every day. The knowledge of the dynamic of the preaching experience in the Hispanic environment will help non-Hispanic preachers to connect with this important group through their preaching.

---

[125]   Davis, 23.

The structure of this study includes the following chapters:

Chapter 2 discusses the methodology of the study, sampling procedures, pilot project, and the description of the research instrument.

Chapter 3 discusses and analyzes the findings of the study.

Chapter 4 provides the conclusions, limitations and recommendations for future researches in this subject.

CHAPTER 2

Methodology

This research project was designed to measure the effect that the independent variable, the models and styles of preaching, has over the dependent variable, the congregations of Hispanic immigrants. The study was conducted among Hispanic clergies, ordained and lay preachers, serving in Hispanic Christian churches in the United States. Each of the clergies included in the sampling is from a Spanish speaking country.

It was hypothesized that preachers in Hispanic churches used a specific style and model of preaching to effectively reach out to the Latino community. In other words, the type of preaching and the way preachers deliver the Word in congregations of Hispanic immigrants influence the reception of the message. The main goal of this research is to assist Non-Hispanic leaders in their efforts to connect through the sermon with the Hispanic community.

Research Design

In order to test the outcome of the most used models and styles of preaching, the study utilized a quasi-experimental design involving a convenience sampling. All of the participants in the study were actively preaching in Hispanic churches in different states in the United States. This study is a quantitative cross-sectional design to explore the opinions of Hispanic clergies of their individual preaching approaches to reach out to Hispanic immigrants living in the United States. According to Rubin and Babbie, cross-sectional studies are based on observations representing a single point in time.[126]

Study Variables

This study examines the relationship between model and styles of preaching and the perceived effectiveness for the reception of the message among Hispanic immigrants who attend Christian churches in different areas of the United States. To examine this relationship, the author examined the following variables:

Dependent Variable

The dependent variable for this study is the perceived reception of the proclaimed Word in Hispanic churches. The author utilized the frequency of implemented models and styles of preaching in Latino congregations to test the dependent variable.

Independent Variable

The author examined two independent variables. The first variable is the preaching model. The preaching model was tested considering the three traditional models that have dominated the understanding of preaching: biblical, rhetorical and relational. The second variable is the preaching style utilized by clergies during their exposition of the Word. The style of preaching refers to the most implemented emphasis during the delivery of the sermon as it complements one of the described models.

---

[126] Allen Rubin and Earl A. Babin, *Research Methods for Social Work*, 5th ed. (Belmont: Thompson Learning, 2006), 248.

Research Questions

This research answers the following questions:

1. What model of preaching is most used by Hispanic clergies in congregations with Latino immigrants?
2. Is there a significant difference among the models of preaching in congregations with Hispanic immigrants?
3. What style of preaching is most used by Hispanic preachers in congregations with Hispanic immigrants?
4. Do Hispanic preachers adjust their sermon based on the cultural background of Hispanic immigrants?
5. What social elements influence the preaching style in the Latino setting?

Hypotheses

The research was guided by two types of hypotheses. The first hypothesis was the research or alternative hypothesis (H1) and the second hypothesis was the null hypothesis (Ho). A research or alternative hypothesis (H1) is a statement that specifies the parameters in one of the following: (a) Not equal to some specified values. (b) Greater than some specialized values (c) Less than some specialized values. The null hypothesis (Ho) is a statement of "no difference" which contradicts the research hypothesis. The null hypothesis usually stated that there is no difference between the mean and some specified values.[127] Based on this classification the researcher proposed the following hypotheses:

1. H1: Hispanic clergies identified the biblical model of preaching as the most frequent, followed by the rhetorical model of preaching. The relational model of preaching is the least frequent model of preaching in Latino congregations.

---

[127] Nachmias C. Frankfort and Guerrero A. Leon, *Social Statistics for a Diverse Society.* 3rd ed. (Thousand Oaks, CA: Pine Forge Press, 2002), 39.

Ho: The Hispanic clergies did not identify significant differences among the three traditional models of preaching in Latino congregations.

2. H1: The style of preaching of Hispanic clergies in congregations with Hispanic immigrants involves the active participation of the congregation.

Ho: The style of preaching of Hispanic clergies in congregations with Hispanic immigrants does not involve the active participation of the congregation.

Unit of Analysis

The unit of analysis for this research was the Hispanic clergies, ordained ministers and lay preachers with experience preaching in Hispanic churches. The research involved thirty-six participants who perform their ministry in areas of high concentration of Hispanic immigrants in the United States.

Inclusion Criterion

The criterion to select the sampling of the study was the preaching ministry of Hispanic lay preachers and Latino ordained ministers in Hispanic churches of the United States. All the participants were born in Spanish-speaking countries including the Caribbean, North, Central, and South America.

Instrument for Data Collection Collect the Data

To assess the opinion of clergies, the researcher designed and administered a questionnaire (See Appendix B) which provided for demographic information, ministry experience, models of preaching and styles of preaching. The questionnaire consisted of forty-two items. The questions were designed to collect data in terms of the frequency that preachers use specific models and styles of preaching in the Hispanic context. Respondents specified their level of agreement with each item on a 4-point scale with higher scores indicating more favorable opinion. The researcher conducted a pilot study to test the instrument for reliability and validity.

Pilot Testing

The research was conducted after testing the instrument in a pilot study. This type of study is a small-scale version of the major study to test the adequacy of the research instruments. The instrument was tested to determine the feasibility and workability of the full-scale study. The pilot project contributed to modify the instrument to collect the data.[128] It was conducted using three subjects. They provided feedback about the questionnaire and proposed some changes to collect the data. Two of the subjects of the pilot project were ordained ministers and the third one was a lay preacher.

The pilot study fulfilled its purpose and helped the researcher to determine the reliability of the questionnaire. As part of the pilot project the researcher interviewed the participants selected for this preliminary assessment. They offered their opinions over the purpose of the study, the difficulty of the instrument and the pertinence of the questions. The preliminary test was instrumental for the modification of the length of instrument and for the review of key questions to collect the data. The interviews contributed to evaluate the feasibility of the study and reinforced the need for the research.

Data Collection Procedure

The initial contact with the participants was via telephone and electronic mail. The researcher requested the cooperation of religious leaders who sent a letter to clergies asking for their involvement. Also,

---

[128] David De Vaus, *Surveys in Social Research* 3rd ed. (London: UCL Press, 1993), 337.

the researcher visited several churches to distribute the questionnaire to preachers in those congregations.

The participants received the questionnaire by electronic mail, in person or by mail. The questionnaire consisted of three measure instruments: the demographic information assessment, the multi-dimensional scale to identify models and styles of preaching in the Hispanic setting and their perception regarding the elements that affect the connection between preachers and the congregation.

The questionnaire included open and closed questions. The participants answered the instrument to collect the data in English or Spanish. Since my intention was to protect confidentiality, the participants did not include their names or personal information in the questionnaire. The researcher was always available to provide instructions, answer questions, and collect the questionnaires.

The availability of the respondents for the research was the main limitation for the collection of the data. There was not a centralized organization that gathers information about Hispanic clergies and Latino churches and the sampling was dispersed across the United States. The dispersion of the sampling presented a difficulty for collection of the data, but the convenience method as proposed for this research facilitated the process.

Sampling Design

The study was conducted implementing non-probability sampling techniques to select the participants. According to Rubin & Babbie, this sampling technique is feasible especially for opinions research.[129] I used the sample based on the availability of the clergies for the research and thirty-six preachers, lay and ordained ministers, agreed to answer the questionnaire.

The sample of the population was selected by convenience using a snowball sampling. This type of sampling is used primary for exploratory purposes in researches on minority populations.[130] This technique allowed for each located subject to contact other subjects.

---

[129] Ibid.

[130] Ibid.

In order to reach out 35-40 subjects, as proposed, the researcher sent a personal letter to the contacted clergies. (See Appendix A)

Data Analysis Procedure

The data collected from this quantitative study were coded and entered into the Statistical Package for Social Sciences (SPSS)[131]for analysis. The researcher used several statistical tests to analyze the variables. The measures of central tendency, variance and standard deviation of the variables were determined using descriptive statistics. The distribution of the variables under study was displayed using cross tabulations. These are usually presented as a contingency table in a matrix format. Cross tabulations show the number of respondents who gave a specific combination of responses. Thus, this measure is used to analyze the results because it indicates which of the models and styles of preaching are more used by Hispanic clergies to address the sermon in congregations with Hispanic immigrants.

The relationship between the models and styles of preaching and the perceived response of the congregation was determined using a Pearson correlation. The Pearson correlation measured the association for interval-ratio variables, reflecting the strength of the linear association between the two variables.[132]

To calculate correlations among the variables, the researcher categorized every item on the scale. Each response ranged from 1-4. The number 1 indicated that the respondent strongly disagreed with the statement and number 4 indicated that the respondent strongly agreed with the statement. The questionnaire arranged seven statements for each of the three models of preaching. Also, the researcher grouped 18 statements related to the style of preaching and three statements were arranged to assess indicators of acceptance of the message by the congregation.

---

[131] D. C Howell, *Statistical Methods for Psychology* 4th ed. (Belmont, CA: Wadsworth Publishing Company, 1997), 253.

[132] Ibid.

Operational Definition of Concepts

The following operational definitions guided the research:

a. Hispanic clergies—Ordained ministers and lay preachers that have developed their ministries in churches in the United States and came from Spanish-speaking Latin American countries from the Caribbean, North, Central, or South America. If they were born in the United States, both of their parents must have been born in a Spanish-speaking countries from the Caribbean, North, Central, or South America.

b. Immigrants—Hispanics living in the United States that came from Spanish-speaking countries from the Caribbean, North, Central or South America.

c. Illegal immigrants—Hispanics living in the United States without official authorization from the U.S. government (and/ or the government of their country of origin) and without the benefits granted to the citizens of the United States.

d. Hispanic or Latino/a—Individuals living in the United States with ancestry from Spanish-speaking countries from the Caribbean, North, Central and South America. In this study, it also refers to a common background of Spanish language and customs.

e. Model of preaching—the emphasis from which preachers analyze the verses of the Bible and the style used when preaching to Latino congregations.

f. Style of preaching—the composition and proclamation of the Word by Hispanic preachers including preparation, structure and delivery of the sermon.

g. Null Hypothesis—establishes that there is not significant relationship among the values under research.

h. Alternative Hypothesis—establishes that there is a significant relationship among the values under research.

i. Perception: Subjective interpretation of preachers on the impact of their sermons in congregations with Hispanics immigrants.

j.   Effectiveness of preaching—The preacher's perception of the response of the congregations as a sign of a successful sermon in congregations with Latino immigrant s. k. Opinion—The subjective statements of Hispanic preachers about the interpretation of the reality, experiences or perceptions related to the impact of their sermons.

Chapter three will present and discuss the findings of the data collected.

CHAPTER 3

Findings and Analysis

CHAPTER 3

Findings and Analysis

The third chapter will present the findings of the research and the analysis from the data collected in order to identify the models and styles of preaching most used by Hispanic clergies in congregations with Hispanic immigrants. This chapter will include demographic information about the participants, assessment of their models and styles of preaching and their criteria to measure effectiveness of the sermon.

Country of Origin, Gender and Age

The Hispanic preachers that answered the questionnaires are from Bolivia, Colombia, Costa Rica, Dominican Republic, Mexico, Panama, Puerto Rico and Venezuela. In terms of gender 83.3 are males and 16.7 percent are females. All the participants are older than 35 years of age. Fifty percent of the respondents are in the group age of 36-50 years old and 36.1 percent comprise the group of 51-64 years. The group ages 65 years and older represents 13.9 percent of the respondents.

Denomination

The sampling included clergies from eleven churches. Table 3 shows the composition of the sampling by religious denomination.

Table 3. Frequency of Participants by Denomination

Denomination	Frequency	Percent	Cumulative Percent
Pentecostal	17	47.2	47.2
Baptist	5	13.9	61.1
Presbyterian	5	13.9	75.0
Adventist	2	5.6	80.6
Methodist	1	2.8	83.4
Catholic	1	2.8	86.2
Evangelic	1	2.8	89.0
Converge	1	2.8	91.8
Restoration	1	2.8	94.6
Assembly Christian	1	2.8	97.4
CLA	1	2.8	100.0

The Pentecostal group comprised sixty-one percent of the sampling. The clergies that belong to mainline churches represented thirty-nine percent of the sampling including a Catholic priest.

Education

The findings revealed that not all the respondents have formal theological education. The education level of the sampling ranges from high school diplomas to doctoral degrees. The majority of the respondents (52.8 percent) that have post-graduate education in areas related to religion such as divinity, ministry, and theology are members of the historical churches. The composition of the sampling included clergies who have bachelor degrees or less.

According to a cross tabulation between education and denomination, 76.4 percent of Pentecostal preachers in the study have a bachelor degree or less; 29.4 percent of this group have a high school diploma. In contrast, the clergies from denominations other that Pentecostal churches that have post—graduate degrees comprised 84.2 percent of the sampling. The findings revealed that the education of 41.6 percent of the respondents is in areas not related to ministry such as engineering, pedagogy, architecture, labor relations, logistics or management.

Those who have a high school diploma received their education in general studies and mechanics. These data validate the literature presented in chapter 1 affirming that education and ordination are not main elements for the authenticity of the preacher in Hispanic congregations. One important distinction of Hispanic congregations is that these communities see the connection to the people and spiritual background of the preacher as key factors for credibility.

Development of Preaching Ministries

The participants for this research were ordained ministers and lay preachers serving in fourteen states of the nation. Table 4 shows geographical location of ministry.

Table 4. Geographical Location of Ministry

State	Frequency	Percent	Valid Percent	Cumulative Percent
California	1	2.8	2.8	2.8
Chicago	1	2.8	2.8	5.6
Colorado	1	2.8	2.8	8.3
Florida	3	8.3	8.3	16.7
Georgia	12	33.3	33.3	50.0
Kentucky	1	2.8	2.8	52.8

Louisiana	6	16.7	16.7	69.4
Maryland	1	2.8	2.8	72.2
Massachusetts	1	2.8	2.8	75.0
N. Carolina	1	2.8	2.8	77.8
New York	2	5.6	5.6	83.4
Rhode Island	2	5.6	5.6	89.0
Texas	1	2.8	2.8	91.8
Virginia	2	5.6	5.6	97.4
n/c	1	2.8	2.8	100.0
Total	36	100.0	100.0	

The ordained ministers represented 61.1 percent of the respondents and 38.9 percent identified themselves as lay preachers. The experience of these two groups performing their ministry ranges from one year to over 40 years of ministry. The majority (47.3 percent) of the preachers serving in the United States have been in ministry at least eleven years and 27.7 percent of the sampling range from 20 years to 42 years of ministry. The average time of preaching for the sampling is 14 years which implies continuity, sense of calling and commitment.

Frequency of Preaching and Language Used

Most of the Hispanic clergies (61.1 percent) preach at least monthly and 44.4 percent of them preach weekly. Other respondents (33.3 percent) expressed that they preach every two months or quarterly. Only one respondent expressed not having the opportunity to preach regularly. Most of them (75.0 percent) preach in Spanish. However, 13.9 percent expressed that they preach in English regardless of the composition of the congregation and 11.1 percent of them accommodate their preaching to different groups preaching in both languages, English and Spanish.

Goals of Preaching

The researcher explored the main goal of preaching in congregations with Latino immigrants. The review of literature suggested that the message of salvation is the primary goal of Hispanic preachers in the proclamation of the Word. The findings sustained this initial observation. In an open-ended question, the respondents validated the topic of salvation as their major goal. The researcher grouped the answers by operational categories. The answers were broken down into the following goals of preaching: evangelistic, doctrinal, encouraging, devotional, consecration and moral. Table 5 reflects the distribution in terms of the categories of the goal of preaching as expressed by Hispanic clergies.

Table 5. Goals of Preaching in Hispanic Congregations

Goal	Frequency	Percent	Valid Percent	Cumulative Percent
Evangelistic	20	55.6	55.6	55.6
Doctrinal	7	19.4	19.4	75.0
Encouraging	3	8.3	8.3	83.3
Devotional	3	8.3	8.3	91.7
Consecration	1	2.8	2.8	94.4
Moral	1	2.8	2.8	97.2
No response	1	2.8	2.8	100.0
Total	36	100.0	100.0	

Some of the typical responses about the goals for the sermon were:
(1) "Present and share Christ."
(2) "Conversion and salvation."
(3) "Gain the people for Christ."
(4) "To integrate the gospel to their lives."

(5) "Glorify Christ and preach salvation."
(6) "Restore, educate and bless Hispanics."
(7) "Salvation, hope, equality for self esteem."
(8) "Spiritual growth, discipleship and evangelism."

The Dominant Preaching Model for Hispanic Immigrants

One of the objectives of this study was to identify the most used models of preaching in the Hispanic context. The researcher selected the biblical, rhetorical and relational models of preaching as defined in the first chapter. To accomplish this purpose, the researcher included seven statements for each model. Respondents did not know the arrangement of the statements or the name of the models in order to avoid suggesting a specific answer. The researcher divided the sum of the total score of the seven statements into the categories more likely and less likely and assigned a value from 7.00 to 28.00. The maximum that a respondent could give as more likely was 28.00 and the minimum for less likely that respondents could have was 7.00.

Therefore, to measure likelihood for the use of a specific model, the score began with the smaller collective value obtained. The answer choices were: strongly agree, agree, disagree and strongly disagree. In these findings, the values ranged from 15.00-28.00 because the majority of the respondents strongly agreed or agreed with all the preaching models. Participants with scores of 15.00-21.00 were labeled to be less likely to use the model. Participants with scores of 22.00-28.00 were labeled more likely to use the model.

The result of the most used model of preaching revealed that respondents were more likely to use the biblical model when preaching to Hispanics immigrants. This model was followed by the rhetorical model, and the relational model was the least likely. The biblical model reached the highest percentage of preference among Hispanic preachers. However, the results suggest that the rhetorical and relational models are part of the preaching experience in the Hispanic environment. The highest value for the use of the biblical model was 27.00 implying that there is not a pure biblical approach of preaching. The values over 22.00 show the biblical model as the dominant approach. However, the high percentage (52.8 percent) under the frequency 20.00-23.00

suggests the presence of the rhetorical and the relational models in the same setting. Table 6 presents the values of the likelihood for the use of the biblical model of preaching

Table 6. Values for the Use of the Biblical Model of Preaching

Model Values	Frequency	Percent	Valid Percent	Cumulative Percent
18.00	3	8.3	8.3	8.3
19.00	3	8.3	8.3	16.7
20.00	6	16.7	16.7	33.3
21.00	4	11.1	11.1	44.4
22.00	6	16.7	16.7	61.1
23.00	3	8.3	8.3	69.4
24.00	6	16.7	16.7	86.1
25.00	1	2.8	2.8	88.9
26.00	3	8.3	8.3	97.2
27.00	1	2.8	2.8	100.0
Total	36	100.0	100.0	

One of the hypotheses of the research was that Hispanic clergies identified the biblical model as the most frequent, followed by the rhetorical model of preaching. The relational model of preaching was the least utilized model of preaching in Latino congregations. Based on these findings the alternative hypothesis (H1) as defined in chapter 2 is accepted while the null hypothesis is rejected. The following statements were selected to assess the use of the biblical model:

(1) "Every sermon for Hispanic must be rooted in the biblical text".

(2) "I follow closely the logic of the biblical text without delineating a theme or thesis".

(3) "The sermon and the Bible have the same authority in the Hispanic setting".

(4) "My sermon emphasizes the meaning of the verses; it is a mouthpiece of the Bible".

(5) "My sermons adhere to a chosen Bible passage with a key verse as a guideline."

(6) "I build my sermons by threading a series of verses of the Bible citing chapter and verses".

(7) "Hispanics expect a biblical, profound and straight-to-the-point message".

Rhetorical Model of Preaching

The rhetorical model of preaching conceives the sermon as a religious performance. It emphasizes the preacher as the main character of the sermon. This model does not exclude the Bible, but the preacher has the freedom to interpret based on his/her own way of thinking and attributes. In this approach, the divine aspect of the sermon is balanced with its persuasive human aspect. In order to assess the rhetorical model, the researcher grouped seven statements that emphasized the personality and feelings of the preacher. The statements were grouped without identifying them in order to avoid the suggestion of a specific answer. Sixty-one percent (61.1%) of the respondents disagreed with the statements related to the rhetorical model in their preaching. Table 7 presents the values for the use of the rhetorical model based on the proposed statements.

Table 7. Values for the Use of the Rhetorical Model of Preaching

Model Values	Frequency	Percent	Valid Percent	Cumulative Percent
17.00	2	5.6	5.6	5.6
18.00	1	2.8	2.8	8.3

19.00	2	5.6	5.6	13.9
20.00	7	19.4	19.4	33.3
21.00	10	27.8	27.8	61.1
22.00	3	8.3	8.3	69.4
23.00	2	5.6	5.6	75.0
24.00	3	8.3	8.3	83.3
25.00	4	11.1	11.1	94.4
26.00	1	2.8	2.8	97.2
27.00	1	2.8	2.8	100.0
Total	36	100.0	100.0	

The respondents strongly agreed or agreed with the use of the rhetorical model, represented over thirty-eight percent (38.8 %). The following statements were selected to assess the likelihood for the use of the rhetorical model:

(1) "In the Latino setting I have authority and freedom to express my personal view of the text."
(2) "The sermon is a performance in which Hispanics expect to be participants."
(3) "My preaching has a personal approach because I show my emotions to connect with the audience."
(4) "I develop my ideas of the text as I preach the sermon."
(5) "My preaching to Hispanics combines theology, gestures, voice and rhetoric."
(6) "I include my personal experiences, points of view and opinions in the sermon."
(7) "I am the one that selects the theme of my sermon and I use the text to sustain it."

The Relational Model of Preaching

The relational model of preaching sees the audience as the main concern of the preacher. In this approach, the context determines the sermon. The researcher included the following seven statements to identify the likelihood for the use of this relational model.

(1) "The situation and the social context dictate the purpose of the sermon I preach."
(2) "I prepare the sermon based on the needs and struggles of Hispanic immigrants."
(3) "My main guideline for a sermon is the current needs of the listeners."
(4) "I avoid using texts that could remind Hispanics of their experiences of fear and suffering."
(5) "Hispanics expect a message of hope and assurance."
(6) "I mention in my sermons illustrations that make sense to the Hispanic culture."
(7) "I use common language of the streets and the market places when preaching to Hispanics."

Table 8 shows the distribution of the values for the relational model of preaching.

Table 8. Values for the Relational Model

Relational model	Frequency	Percent	Valid Percent	Cumulative Percent
15.00	1	2.8	2.8	2.8
16.00	1	2.8	2.8	5.6
18.00	6	16.7	16.7	22.2
19.00	3	8.3	8.3	30.6
20.00	6	16.7	16.7	47.2
21.00	3	8.3	8.3	55.6

22.00	6	16.7	16.7	72.2
23.00	3	8.3	8.3	80.6
24.00	3	8.3	8.3	88.9
25.00	1	2.8	2.8	91.7
26.00	1	2.8	2.8	94.4
27.00	1	2.8	2.8	97.2
28.00	1	2.8	2.8	100.0
Total	36	100.0	100.0	

It is significant that 55.6 percent of the respondents are less likely to use the relational model in the Hispanic environment. Those who are more likely to use the relational model, 44.4 percent, fall between the values 22.00 and 24.00. The data suggest that preachers use the relational model in combination with both the biblical model and the rhetorical approach of preaching.

Opinion of Their Own Model of Preaching

The research included an open-ended question about the opinion that clergies have in terms of their personal model of preaching. The purpose of the question was to validate their previous response about the three models of preaching. The study asked the respondents to describe their model of preaching. It is significant that 22.2 percent did not answer the question. Other respondents did not refer directly to their models of preaching and described their models of preaching using words such as "paternalist," "direct and right to the point," and "passionate." Only twenty-two percent of the respondents identified their models of preaching in terms of our operational definitions of biblical, rhetorical or contextual. In this group, the biblical model was the most mentioned approach to preaching. The majority of the respondents (61.1 percent) were not able to identify their own models of preaching.

Styles of Preaching in Congregations of Hispanic Immigrants

One of the main purposes of the research was to assess data about the preaching styles in congregations with Latino immigrants. The objective was to explore the styles of preaching in relation to the involvement of the congregation as part of the preaching experience. The alternative hypothesis (H1), as defined in the second chapter, proposed that preachers actively involved the congregation in their preaching styles. In order to assess this objective, the researcher included eighteen statements designed to collect information about styles of preaching. The respondents evaluated their preaching styles based on what they do and what they think the congregation expects from them. The statements included the process of preparation of the sermon, construction of the sermon, and delivery of the sermon.

Also, the research included three statements to measure the ways Hispanic preachers receive feedback from the congregation. The study revealed that the style of preaching for the Hispanic immigrant community is participatory and confirmed the alternative hypothesis establishing that Hispanic preachers actively involved the congregation in their preaching styles. Therefore, the alternative hypothesis (H1) is accepted and the null hypothesis is rejected. The findings on the topic about the styles of preaching in the Hispanic community are discussed in the sections that follow.

Preparation and Construction of the Sermon

According to the data collected, preachers in the Hispanic setting are unprompted. Over 65.7 percent of the respondents expressed that they do not write their own sermon. Some of them use an outline but the majority (61.1 percent) develops their ideas as they preach. They construct the sermon based on direct use of the Bible. The respondents (74.2 percent) build their sermons by using several verses of the Bible quoting chapters and verses. Only one person, representing 5.7 percent completely disagrees with this type of construction of the sermon. Most of the participants preach sermons that have an introduction, central points and conclusion. The method of preaching to the majority of them (88.8 percent) is the inductive method that moves from a general truth toward a particular conclusion. The deductive method of preaching that moves from a particular experience toward a general truth was clearly rejected by 31.4 percent of the respondents.

The Use of the Lectionary and the Bible

According to the findings, Hispanic clergies do not use the lectionary as a preaching tool even though the biblical model is their most used model of preaching. Only 5.8 percent completely agreed with the use of the lectionary for preparation of the sermon while the majority (76.4 percent) completely disagreed with the use of this means. It is significant that 83.3 percent select the theme of their sermon first and then use the biblical text to sustain the theme selected. The use of the Bible during preaching in the Hispanic community is essential and 100.0 percent believe that every sermon must be rooted in the biblical text.

Delivery of the Sermon

The delivery of the sermon in the Hispanic environment is dynamic and connectional. The majority of the respondents (61.0 percent) ask questions from the Bible to the congregation to keep them engaged. They believe that anecdotes and jokes are essential to make the sermon personal. A high percentage of 88.8 expressed that they tell anecdotes and jokes as an integral part of the sermon. The study revealed that Hispanic preachers give their preaching a personal touch showing to the congregations their emotions. A significant 63.8 percent validated the statement "My preaching has a personal approach because I show my emotions to connect with the audience."

As a way to connect with the audience, Hispanic preachers (77.0 percent) illustrate their sermons with dramatizations of the biblical text. Connection to the audience is also through the use of popular language. The majority of the respondents (51.3percent) use common language of the street and market place when preaching to Hispanics.

However, 27.7 percent disagreed and 11.1 completely rejected the use of common language of the street and market place in preaching. The researcher infers that the fact that Spanish varies from culture to culture presents a challenge to preachers because they want to be sure that the message is clearly understood by all Hispanic people.

Preaching in churches of Hispanic immigrants tends to be lengthy. The majority of the respondents (55.0 percent) preach more than thirty minutes. However, the fact that 44.4 percent disagreed with the statement in terms of the extent of the sermon reflects that there is not a generalized consensus for the duration of a sermon. As expressed in the first chapter, the effort to keep the interest of the audience requires time and it might be reflected in the time dedicated to preaching.

Also, as part of the delivery of the sermon, preachers move away from the pulpit during preaching. The majority (71.4 percent) of the respondents agreed that they move away from the pulpit and closer to the people. Only 2.8 percent completely disagreed with this action as part of the delivery of their sermon. Answering a subjective question the clergies described their preaching styles as: "dynamic," "personal," "flexible," "interactive," "emotional" and "joyful with authority." All these descriptions confirm the findings related to styles of preaching included in the structured questions as indicated.

Prayer is evidently present during the delivery of the sermon. Almost all the respondents (97.2 percent) expressed that they always pray with the congregation before delivering a sermon. This percentage was validated by the statement "My sermon includes prayer at the end and the altar call" in which 94.4 percent strongly agreed with this statement.

Besides prayer, the Hispanic preachers sometimes invite the congregation to sing before, during or after the sermon. This practice of singing with the congregation as part of the preaching experience was sustained by 65.7 percent. This percentage reflects that some Hispanic preachers consider singing an important piece of a successful experience in the pulpit. It is significant that not one of the respondents completely disagreed with the statement about the practice of singing before, during or after the sermon. Clergies and lay preachers representing 94.4 percent of the respondents agreed that the sermon must conclude with an altar call.

Reception of the Sermon by the Congregation

One of the questions that guided this study intended to explore the way Hispanic preachers perceive the response to the sermon. The researcher included three statements in the instrument to collect the data to identify indicators to measure acceptance or effectiveness of a sermon. The statements were directed to explore physical responses, verbal signs and emotional responses to preaching. The first declaration to assess the physical response from the congregations was: "Gesture, rising of hands, tears, and laughter are signs that the sermon has been effective."

Table 9 presents the findings in terms of physical responses as a sign of approval.

Table 9 Physical Response as a Sign of Approval

Response	Frequency	Percentage	Cumulative
Strongly Agree	9	25.0	25.0
Agree	14	38.8	63.8
Disagree	11	30.5	94.3
Strongly disagree	2	5.5	100.0

Table 9 suggests that the majority of the respondents (65.0 percent) considered that gestures, rising of hands, tears and laughter are evident physical responses of the effectiveness of a sermon. The data suggest that a third part of the sampling do not perceive physical expressions as a sign of effectiveness.

The research explored the verbal expression as a demonstration of validation of a sermon. Hispanic preachers recognize the participation of the congregation during preaching. They perceive that the request to keep preaching is a clear indication that God is speaking to the congregation through them. They receive the encouragement from the congregation as a message to extend the time of preaching. This factor influences the length of the sermon because Hispanic preachers know that a sermon over thirty minutes is acceptable in this environment.

Table 10 presents the findings regarding the response to the statement "Hispanics encourage the preacher to extend the time of the sermon if they feel that God is talking to them."

Table 10. Verbal Signs of Effectiveness for a Sermon

Response	Frequency	Percentage	Cumulative
Strongly Agree	8	22.2	22.2
Agree	21	58.3	80.5
Disagree	7	19.4	100.0
Strongly disagree	0	0	100.0

Another indicator of the effectiveness of the sermon for the sampling is the response to the altar call. According to 58.3 percent, the acceptance to the invitation to the altar is a sign of success. Table 11 groups the answers to the statement "In Hispanic congregations the response to the altar call is a good indicator of the effectiveness of the sermon."

Table 11. Emotional Sign of Effectiveness of the Sermon

Response	Frequency	Percentage	Cumulative
Strongly Agree	8	22.2	22.2
Agree	13	36.1	58.3
Disagree	14	38.1	96.4
Strongly disagree	1	2.7	100.0

It is significant that only 2.7 percent strongly disagreed with the statement in terms of the invitation to the altar. The fact that the respondents perceive the acceptance of the invitation to the altar as a sign of effectiveness moves them to end their sermon with an altar call and prayer as previously discussed. Hispanic preachers who link the sermon and the altar call as one unit spend a long time trying to persuade the people to come forward because they feel that the message failed if nobody accepts the invitation to the altar at the end of the sermon.

Main Concerns of Preachers in Hispanic Congregations

The research explored through an open-ended question the main concerns of Hispanic preachers when preach to Hispanic immigrants. The answer was categorized in five major concerns. The breakdown of the responses is presented in Table 12. It is significant that the majority of the respondents expressed concern about the clear understanding of the message by the community. The researcher infers that Hispanic preachers are compelled to search for common words to avoid misunderstanding because the meaning of some words in Spanish varies by culture.

The fact that the clear understanding of the message is one of the major concerns of Hispanic preachers influences the way they prepare and deliver the sermon. This might be the reason to explain why preachers use common language of the street and market place and dramatize their sermon as previously revealed.

Another major concern of Hispanic preachers is to be effective responding to the spiritual needs of the community with a percentage of 22.2. The fulfillment of the cultural needs was also mentioned as a major concern of the sampling.

The participants pointed out diversity of the community and the meaning of the words by the different cultures as the reasons for their concern over understanding of the message. One of the respondents expressed concern that to be misunderstood in some way might denigrate some cultures. The meaning of some words in the Hispanic environment is linked to the cultural background of the members of the congregation and varies depending on the Hispanic countries. The same word that is correct in one country might be offensive in another country and in some cases the words have the opposite meanings.

The research revealed that the satisfaction of the spiritual needs of the audience is another concern of Hispanic preachers because they want to bring hope, encouragement and consolation to the community. Bringing a clear gospel message so that the community could feel that God has not forsaken the Hispanic immigrants and suffers with them is one of the major concerns of Hispanic preachers. The satisfaction of the cultural and social needs of the immigrants was a concern of 13.8 percent of the respondents.

It is significant that some of the participants declared their concern of not being effective in helping the Hispanic immigrants to overcome their crises, their grief and pain. The adjustment and inclusion of Hispanic immigrants as part of culture in the United States was also a concern revealed in the study. Table 12 presents the main concerns as expressed by Hispanic preachers.

Table 12. Main Concern of Hispanic Preachers

Concern	Frequency	Percent	Cumulative Percent
Understanding of the Word	16	44.4	44.4
Fulfilling the spiritual needs	8	22.2	66.6
Fulfilling the cultural needs	5	13.8	80.4
Moving Hispanics to salvation	2	5.5	85.9
No concern at all	2	5.5	91.4
No response	3	8.3	100.0

As Table 12 shows, the spiritual welfare is the major concern of Hispanic preachers. The fact that 5.5 percent expressed having no concern at all and 8.3 percent did not respond to the question suggests that some Hispanic preachers are not aware of the spiritual, social and cultural needs of this particular community.

The final chapter will present the conclusions and the recommendations. It also will include some recommendations offered by Hispanic clergies to reach out to the Latino community through preaching.

CHAPTER 4

Conclusions, Limitations and Recommendations

CHAPTER 4

Conclusions, Limitations and Recommendations

Conclusions

Immigration of Hispanics is one of the most important issues in the United States and it is affecting the church in this country. The interaction of Christian churches with the Hispanic community demands an intentional preaching ministry. This research was conducted to offer general guidance on how to connect with Hispanic immigrants through preaching.

Preaching is essential in order to fulfill an integral worship experience for the spiritual growth of Hispanics in this country. The unique reality of this community demands a clear understanding and sense of purpose of preaching. Preaching as an act of ministry promotes the spiritual transformation and the social growth of the people so it must be intentional especially as it is meant to be relevant to the Hispanic context. The presence of Latinos in the United States challenges the mission of the church because Hispanics are the fastest growing minority in this nation.

This study was designed to assess the models and styles of preaching of Hispanic preachers in order to provide empirical data to Non-Hispanic clergies; thus, they can meet the challenge that the phenomenon of Hispanic immigration represents. The research reveals information related to the experience, insight and opinions of Hispanic clergies on their ways to connect with the Latino community and the signs to understand the behavior of this group during worship.

Hispanic immigrants attending the congregations in the United States have common issues. Many of them need work, shelter, interpersonal connections, physical care, emotional adjustment, and spiritual guidance. Others confront trouble adapting to the pressure of this country due to lack of English as a second language. Some Hispanic immigrants bring to the church their fears, frustration and their anxieties. All these feelings impact the way Hispanics worship and listen to the sermon. Preaching for Hispanic congregations is a communal act. In worship they integrate their daily experiences and expect a direct connection with preachers through the sermon.

The act of preaching is an encounter between the people and the preacher beyond a manuscript. Worship in this environment demands the interaction between the preacher and the congregation. The task to preach effectively to people living in the situation of many Hispanics is not easy. A typical congregation will have a mixture of Hispanics from various countries, diverse levels of acculturation, and histories of suffering and religious background.

The act of preaching in the Latino setting is participative and personal; thus preachers must have credibility and connection. Credibility is based on their religious background, credentials and personal testimony. Connection implies that the congregation perceives that preachers share its same cultural values. The power of solidarity is essential because preachers comfort, affirm and challenge the spiritual growth of the people. Credibility, connection and solidarity are important for the best receptivity of the message. Hispanic congregations are responsive and give feedback to confirm the acceptance of the preacher and the message.

Preachers in this setting should know how to recognize and respond to the dynamics in this congregation. The various groups within the same congregation have different expectations, needs, experiences, and perceptions that challenge the preachers. Therefore, it is important to identify the approaches to preaching that better suit the needs and uniqueness of the Hispanic community.

This research concluded that the biblical model of preaching is the most dominant approach to preaching even though it is not mutually exclusive to the other two models: the rhetorical and the relational. Also, the study revealed that the style of preaching in the Hispanic setting is participatory because the congregation has an active role during preaching. These two main findings will be discussed in this final chapter.

Profile of a Hispanic Preacher

According to the sampling, a typical Hispanic preacher is male and older than 35 years. The education background is diverse and it is directly linked to the requirements of the preacher's religious denomination. Preachers who have bachelor's degree or less are related to the Pentecostal church. Those that have master's degrees or doctoral degrees in areas related to religion such as divinity, ministry, and theology are members of mainline churches.

The research discovered that not all the preachers in the Hispanic church possess formal theological education. They function as ordained ministers or lay leaders. Also, a college degree is not essential for a preacher's role in the Latino setting. The average length of active ministry is fourteen years. Hispanic clergies typically preach mostly in Spanish on a weekly basis.

Goal of Preaching of Hispanic Clergies

The research explored the main goal of preaching in the Hispanic religious setting and revealed that the evangelistic purpose drives clergies when they address the Latino immigrants through preaching. This conclusion is supported by the literature suggesting that the message of salvation is the key concern of Hispanic preachers in the Latino congregations.

Model of Preaching

One of the goals of the study was to explore the most used model of preaching by Hispanic clergies in Latino congregations. The research concluded that the biblical model is the most used model of preaching followed by the rhetorical model and then the relational model of preaching. However, the study also revealed that the use of these three models is not mutually exclusive because there is overlapping among the three traditional models of preaching.

The consensus for the use of the biblical model is explicit. Hispanic preachers think that the sermon is the Word of God and in the Hispanic context it has the same authority as the Bible. They believe that every sermon must be rooted in the biblical text. In their approach to the biblical text, Hispanic preachers closely follow the logic of the verses without delineating a theme or thesis. Preachers build their sermons by putting together a series of verses of the Bible, citing chapters and verses. They consider that the sermon is a mouthpiece of the Bible.

However, the degree of influence that the rhetorical model seems to have over the biblical approach is significant. Hispanic preachers are active subjects of the sermon and make preaching a personal craft. Their sermons combine theology, gestures, voice and rhetoric.

Latino preachers show their emotions in their sermons and express with freedom their personal point of view of the text. Some of them consider the sermon a performance. This overlap is significant because the personal approach of Hispanic preachers makes the sermon a rhetorical piece even though they clearly believe that their sermons are totally biblical.

The relational model was the less likely model to be used by Hispanic preachers. The emphasis of this model is on the hearers. Their needs move the topic of the message. Those most likely to use this approach of preaching stated that the situation and the social context dictate the purpose of the sermon. They see the current needs of the listeners as the main guideline for their sermons and prepare their sermons based on the needs and struggles of the Hispanic community.

However, the three models share some common ground. The three models of preaching consider that the sermon for Hispanic immigrants must be direct and straight to the point. Also, preachers should not avoid using texts that could remind Hispanics of their experiences of fear and suffering.

Styles of Preaching

One of the objectives of the study was to assess the preaching style in the Hispanic setting. The research explored the proclamation of the Word by Hispanic preachers including preparation, structure and delivery of the sermon.

The study revealed that the style of preaching for Hispanic immigrants is participatory because preachers develop a direct, personal and connectional style. Ilion T. Jones referred to this type of style of preaching as "aural style." The word "aural" literally means of or "pertaining to the ears." He accepts also the concept "shirt sleeves" style because it means that is tailored to the needs of the listeners.[133] According to Jones, this style provides preachers their direct path to the minds, hearts, consciences, and wills of listeners.[134]

Structure of the Sermon

Structure makes a sermon strong and it includes both the pattern of preparation and the composition in terms of its parts. The study revealed that Hispanic clergies preach inductive sermons. They develop the sermon from a general truth toward specific experiences. According to Fred B. Craddock, the inductive preaching tests several possibilities and narrows to a conclusion.[135] Hispanic clergies narrow their conclusions to accomplish the purpose of salvation as their main goal for the sermon, as revealed by the research.

Hispanic congregations expect a message based on direct use of the Bible. Preachers in this setting must use the Bible as their primary source. Mentioning verses of the Bible by quoting chapters and verses to reinforce a point of the sermon is essential for a successful sermon. The study revealed that regardless of the model of preaching, the preacher must let the congregation know before the sermon the verses of the Scriptures for the message. The use of the Bible is essential before going outside the Scriptures for reference. However, the use of the lectionary to select the verses for preaching is not a popular tool among preachers in the Hispanic setting.

The research revealed that sermons for Hispanic immigrants have a structure. Charles W. Koller states that structure can make the difference

---

133 Jones, 174.

134 Ibid.

135 Wilson, 11.

between futility and effectiveness in a sermon. A sound structure provides the preacher with a sense of timing, progress and proportion and helps the congregation to follow the ideas of the preacher.[136] In terms of structure, the study revealed that the sermons of Hispanic clergies have an introduction, central points and a conclusion.

Delivery of the Sermon

The delivery of the sermon is the most important way to communicate the Word of God. According to Ilion T. Jones, a sermon exists only when it has been delivered. Not until it has been preached can its function of communicating the gospel be fulfilled.[137] The manner of delivery is a key factor for the success of the sermon. Preachers have exclusive control over the style involved in their method of delivery. The researcher distinguished four types of sermon delivery for the purpose of this study: free preaching, reading the sermon from a manuscript, preaching using an outline and reciting the sermon from memory.

The research revealed that preachers in the Hispanic setting do not write their sermons. Preaching from a manuscript was the least acceptable option. Preachers in the Hispanic setting preach freely, without notes, and develop their ideas as they preach. The practice of preaching using an outline is also accepted. Reading a sermon affects adversely the interaction because eyes contact is essential to connect with the hearers.

The study discovered that the style of preaching for Hispanic clergies is participatory. The behavior of Hispanic preachers influences the way they deliver their sermons. They sing with the congregation before or during the sermon. During the sermon, preachers ask questions to the congregation from the Bible to connect with them. They encourage the congregation to recite verses of the Bible along with them to demonstrate participation from the congregation. Preachers promote this type of behavior from the pulpit because it is acceptable

---

[136] Charles W. Koller, *How to Preach Without Notes,* 2nd ed. (Grand Rapids, Michigan: Baker Books, 2008), 41.

[137] Jones, 186.

by the congregation. Also, in the Hispanic congregations, preachers show their emotions and bring their own points of view and personal opinions in the sermon.

The research showed that preaching beyond thirty minutes is acceptable in the Latino religious environment. In order to keep the attention of the audience, preachers develop a style that promotes an informal environment. Sometimes preachers in the Hispanic setting dramatize the sermon to make it clearer. It is a general behavior to tell anecdotes and jokes as an essential part of the sermon. The illustrations that preachers use during the sermon are related to the Hispanic culture. One of the biggest concerns of Hispanic preachers is to be understood by the audience. In the Hispanic culture, the Spanish spoken varies from culture to culture. The purpose of the preachers is to project an idea from their own minds into the minds of others. The fact that they want to be understood by the different Hispanic groups within the church compels them to speak straight to the point using common language of the street and marketplace in their preaching.

In the Latino worship environment, preachers are encouraged to move away from the pulpit to be closer to the people. This action helps the preacher to connect with the congregation and to reinforce its interaction. Another characteristic of the preaching experience is the centrality of prayer. Preachers must pray before and after the sermon. Prayer is part of the sermon. It is important to start the sermon with prayer and to close it with prayer. Hispanic immigrants expect this type of behavior from the preacher.

Reception of the Message

Hispanic immigrants are responsive during the time of preaching. The research revealed that Hispanic preachers receive feedback from the congregation by different manners. Gestures, raising of hands, tears and laughter are signs that the sermon has been effective. Also, the congregation encourages the preacher to continue the message if they feel that God is speaking to them through the preacher.

Preachers must pay attention to the involvement of the congregation because it will help to successfully conclude the sermon. Success in the Hispanic congregations means that people accept the message and respond to the invitation to the altar. The altar call is part of the sermon. The congregation expects the preacher to ask them to come forward. The research revealed that the response to the altar call is another indicator to measure participation, connection and success of the sermon.

Limitations

This research was conducted to identify the most used models and styles of preaching in congregations with Hispanic immigrants. In the process of conducting the investigation, the researcher recognized that the limitations expressed below made the research process more difficult but did not affect the reliability of the investigation neither altered the findings of the research.

1. Need for a centralized organization: One of the limitations for the study was the absence of a centralized organization to gather information about Hispanic churches in the United States. Because of this limitation the respondents were selected by snowball as defined in the methodology. This process of contacting the sampling required additional time. Also, respondents did not answer the questionnaires on time and it was necessary to extend the time for them to respond. Some of the respondents did not know how to answer questionnaires electronically and required individual attention from the researcher.

2. Need for research on the subject: The researcher faced the limitation of a lack of research on the subject of preaching models and preaching styles in the Hispanic environment. The researcher could not find studies available about the role of preaching in congregations of Hispanic immigrants.

Recommendations

These recommendations have two parts. The first part is related to recommendations based on the experience of Hispanic preachers to help non-Hispanic clergies to reach out to Latino immigrants. The second part has general recommendations based on the result of the research.

Recommendations from Hispanic Preachers

The last question asked Hispanic preachers to provide recommendations to non-Hispanic preachers based on their experience on how to reach out to the Latino immigrants living in the United States. The following are the recommendations from the Hispanic preachers to non-Hispanic leaders to help them to be effective in their efforts to connect with Hispanic immigrants through preaching.[138]

1. "Non-Hispanic clergies must interact with the people."
2. "Non-Hispanic preachers should preach the Word of God with conviction and sincerity of heart. They must say what God wants to say to His people."
3. "Non-Hispanic clergies need to attend to the invitations to eat and socialize. Hispanics function around the table."
4. "Non-Hispanic clergies should provide the moral, social, economic and spiritual support. They must share the grace, love, peace, and hope in Christ."
5. "It is important for non-Hispanic preachers to learn the language, socialize with Hispanics and to know their culture."
6. "Non-Hispanic clergies need to know the Hispanic culture, their customs, the language, in order to identify with them. It is important to be aware of the physical, spiritual and material needs of Hispanic immigrants and look for ways to supply them."
7. "Non-Hispanic clergies should study about the needs of Hispanics in the United States."
8. "Non-Hispanic preachers must emphasize that God does not make a distinction among the people. God loves Hispanic

---

[138] The researcher translated to English some of the recommendations that Hispanic clergies expressed in Spanish.

immigrants and wants them to repent and to be obedient to His Word."

9. "Non-Hispanic clergies need to provide economic support, food and to know the situation of the family. They must show love and interest for the kids, eat with Hispanics and celebrate special events with them."

10. "Non-Hispanic clergies need to get familiar with the different cultures, including words that could have different meanings in other Hispanic countries."

11. "Non Hispanic clergies need to work with the Hispanic community in order to see their urgent needs."

12. "The preaching of non-Hispanic preachers must be alive, biblical and truthful."

13. "Non-Hispanic preachers must keep in mind that the Hispanic community is comprised by people of different colors and races united by a particular language, Spanish, and the love of God in their hearts."

14. "Non-Hispanic clergies should associate with Hispanic immigrants and get involved in their cultural environment in order to understand their struggles with racism and rejection. They must be interested in the news related to Hispanics to develop understanding and mercy in their sermons."

15. "Non-Hispanic preachers should learn how to read the verse of the Bible from the Hispanic immigrant's context and to know the needs of the audience."

16. "It is important for Non-Hispanic preachers to accommodate their message in order to be congruent with the needs of the Hispanic community. It is not possible to preach to Hispanics with a "white" theology."

17. "It is important to immerse yourself in the life situation of the hearers. Be honest about your own failures and weaknesses. Always speak the truth as you believe it and especially as you live it."

18. "Non-Hispanic preachers should dedicate time to learn how to identify the needs of the people and the community in which God has placed them."

19. "Non-Hispanic clergies should be filled of the Holy Spirit, love God and His people."

20. "It is important to be part of the experiences of the immigrants to understand their struggles and suffering while they are trying to serve God. The preaching has to be embodied and assimilated in order to reach the audience. Prepare a sermon based on the context of the preacher, the audience and the text."

21. "Non-Hispanic clergies should take care of the diction, communication and must be practical."

22. "Non-Hispanic clergies must be sincere, present and empathetic with the needs of Hispanics. They must live out what they preach so that they may have credibility within the Latino community."

23. "Non-Hispanic preachers should pray and look for the direction of God."

24. "Non-Hispanic preachers need to learn and respect the distinct cultures and nationalities. They must believe what they preach and use a simple language. They should translate difficult terms and keep a sense of equality. Do not be arrogant but humble in the pulpit. Do not be paternalistic because of your education level or because the congregation perceives that the preacher has a superior culture or class. Share in their homes as the clergies do with their own people. Practice the ministry in the streets and not behind the desk. Minister to the needs and learn the names of the people."

25. "Non-Hispanic clergies need to take time to understand the culture and the Hispano-American theology so they could understand what the Hispanic immigrants demand from a sermon. Hispanics are traditional and conservative."

26. "Non-Hispanic clergies should have a translator and should invite Hispanic preachers to their churches."

27. "Non-Hispanic clergies should learn the ways Hispanics behave. They must pray with them and associate with them."

28. "Non-Hispanic preachers should learn about the experiences of Hispanic immigrants. Use illustrations from the context of the immigrants and not from the preacher's context."

29. "It is important for Non-Hispanic clergies to get involved with the community and to know their idiosyncrasies."

30. "Preachers in the United States should learn how Hispanic immigrants think in terms of religion in order to be effective."

Recommendations for Non-Hispanic Clergies from the Research

The research intended to provide guidance to Non-Hispanic religious leaders on how to reach out to Hispanic immigrants living in the United States. The following are some recommendations as a result of this research:

1. Before accepting the responsibility to preach in the Hispanic environment, every preacher must learn about the Hispanic culture and the differences among Hispanics.

2. Non-Hispanic preachers who are invited to preach in congregations with Hispanic immigrants must be ready to preach as least thirty minutes. Hispanic churches consider that less than thirty minutes is not enough time to preach the Word of God.

3. It is important for preachers to send a clear message to the congregation that they believe in the Scriptures as the Word of God.

4. The Hispanic congregation would like to hear a message on the gospel. The preaching must present a message of salvation. It is important to preach with joy a message of hope and assurance.

5. Every preacher must deliver the message with conviction and authority. Always support the message by mentioning verses of the Bible, quoting chapter and verses.

6. Every preacher should make illustrations an essential part of the sermon. However, it is important to be sure that the anecdotes, jokes or illustrations are adequate for the different Hispanic groups that attend to the church. In case of doubt, it is better to avoid those illustrations.

7. In the Hispanic setting, preachers can show their emotions and feelings. Hispanic immigrants expect to see that the preacher

is a human being who can relate to them. The perception of the congregation is basic to achieve the connection between the preacher and the congregation.

8. Manuscripts are not popular in the Hispanic pulpit. Preachers should not read the manuscript of the sermon word by word. The congregation expects the preacher to connect with each of them through eye contact.

9. It is a normal behavior in congregations of Hispanic immigrants that the preacher moves away from the pulpit during preaching to be closer to the congregation. Preachers in this environment are allowed to have a conversation with the congregation and to ask questions to ensure the effective receptivity of the message.

10. In the Hispanic setting, the congregation reacts to the message during the sermon. In some cases, people express their feelings and their involvement by raising their hands, laughing or crying. That is an acceptable behavior in congregations of Hispanic immigrants.

11. Preachers must be respectful all the time to the sensibility of the worship community. However, the congregation expects the preacher to be direct and straight to the point during the time of preaching.

12. The Hispanic congregation expects the preacher to pray. Prayer is important before the beginning of the sermon and prayer is important after the sermon. Sometimes it is acceptable in the Hispanic environment to pray during the sermon if the preacher feels the need to pray with the congregation.

13. The altar call is part of the sermon in Latino churches. Preachers must end their sermons with an altar call. The people expect the opportunity to go to the altar after hearing a sermon in which they feel God spoke to them. Every preacher in this environment should offer the opportunity to the congregation to accept the invitation to the altar.

APPENDICES

Empirical Opinion of Christian Hispanic Clergies About Their Most Effective Model and Style of Preaching to Reach Out Hispanic Immigrants Living in the United States

QUESTIONNAIRE

Dear Clergy,

This investigation will help non Hispanic clergies to reach out effectively, through preaching, Hispanic immigrants that attend Christian churches in the United States. While your participation is desired, it is entirely voluntary.

I encourage you to share your experiences and perspective on this important topic. I assure you that your response will be kept confidential.

Thank you for your time and assistance in this effort. For more information on this questionnaire, please contact me by e-mail to: pjriveramadera@yahoo.com

Very respectfully,

Pablo Rivera Madera

I. DEMOGRAPHIC INFORMATION:

1. Country of Origin: _____
2. Denomination: _____
3. Age group: (_20-25) (_26-35) (_36-50) (_51 64) (_65-More)
4. Gender: _Male   _Female
5. Education: _High School or less   _Associate degree BA MA DR
6. Major area of study: _____
7. Are you: Ordained clergy?_   _Lay preacher?   _How long?
8. How long you have been preaching in the U.S.? _____
9. Where in the U.S. are you developing your preaching ministry? _____
10. How often do you preach to Hispanics? _____
11. In what language do you most frequently preach?_____
12. What is your main goal when preaching to Hispanics? _____

PREACHING APPROACH FOR HISPANIC IMMIGRANTS:

How much do you agree or disagree with the following statement about your approach to preaching to Hispanic immigrants? (Mark one answer for each statement)

	Strongly agree	Agree	Disagree	Strongly disagree
1. My preaching to Hispanics combines theology, gestures, voice and rhetoric.				
2. I include my personal experiences, point of views and opinions in the sermon.				
3. I am the one that select the theme of my sermon and I use the text to sustain it.				
4. The situation and the social context dictate the purpose of the sermon I preach.				

	Strongly agree	Agree	Disagree	Strongly disagree
5. I prepare my sermons base on the needs and the struggles of Hispanics in the U.S.				
6. I mention in my sermons illustrations that make sense for Hispanic culture.				
7. I agree with Hispanics that the sermon is Word of God.				
8. I prepare my sermons using the lectionary.				
9. Every sermon for Hispanics must be rooted in the Biblical text.				
10. I write my sermons and read directly from the manuscript.				
11. During the sermon I ask questions from the Bible to the congregation to connect with them and to make them participants				
12. I tell anecdotes and jokes as essential part of the sermon in the Hispanic setting.				
13. Hispanics expect a biblical profound, joyful and straight to the point.				
14. Hispanics expect a message of hope and assurance.				
15. I avoid using texts that could remind Hispanics of their experiences of fear, and suffering.				
16. My main guideline for a sermon is the current needs of the listeners.				
17. My sermon moves from a general truth toward specific experiences.				

18. My sermon moves from a particular experience toward a general truth.				
19. The sermons I preach have an introduction, central points and conclusion.				
20. I use common language of the street and marketplace when preaching to Hispanics.				
21. I do not write my sermon but I always prepare an outline to preach to Hispanics.				
22. I develop my ideas of the text as I preach the sermon.				
23. I always write my sermon but I don't read it when preaching to Hispanics				
24. I follow closely the logic of the biblical text without delineate a theme or theses.				
25. I delineate a theme or thesis as a guideline when study the biblical text.				
26. Usually I preach more than thirty minutes in Hispanic congregations.				
27. I build my sermons by threading a series of verses of the Bible citing chapter and verses.				
28. My preaching has a personal approach because I show my emotions to connect with the audience.				
29. Sometimes I invite the congregation to sing before, during or after the sermon.				
30. I always pray with the congregation before delivering a sermon.				

	Strongly agree	Agree	Disagree	Strongly disagree
31. Sometimes I illustrate my sermons with a dramatization of the biblical text.				
32. When I preach I move away out from the pulpit and closer to the people.				
33. Hispanics recite along with the preacher some verses of the Bible as a sign of active participation.				
34. The sermon and the Bible have the same authority in the Hispanic setting.				
35. My sermons adhere to a chosen Bible passage with a key verse as a guideline.				
36. My sermon emphasizes the meaning of the verses and it is a mouthpiece of the Bible.				
37. In the Latino setting I have authority and freedom to express personal point of view of the text.				
38. The sermon is a performance in which Hispanics expect to be participants.				
39. My sermon includes prayer at the end and the altar call.				
40. Gesture, rising of hands, tears and laughter are signs that the sermon has been effective.				
41. Hispanics encourage the preacher to extend the time of the sermon if they feel that God is talking to them.				
42. In Hispanic congregations the response to the altar call is a good indicator of the effectiveness of the sermon.				

What is your major concern when preaching to Hispanic immigrants?

_____

How do you describe your model of preaching? _____

How do you describe your style of preaching?_____

What recommendations can you offer to non-Hispanic preachers that want to reach out to the Latino immigrants living in the United States?

_____

_____

_____

Opinión de Cleros Cristianos Hispanos Sobre Su Propio Modelo y Estilo de Predicación para Alcanzar a Inmigrantes Hispanos que Viven en los Estados Unidos

CUESTIONARIO

Estimado/a Clérigo,

Esta investigación ayudará a cleros no hispanos a alcanzar con eficacia, por medio de la predicación, los inmigrantes hispanos que asisten iglesias cristianas en los Estados Unidos. Su participación es apreciada y es completamente voluntaria.

Le invito a compartir sus experiencias en beneficio de la comunidad hispana. Le aseguro que su respuesta será manejada de forma confidencial.

Gracias por su tiempo y ayuda en este esfuerzo. Para más información sobre este cuestionario, por favor comuníquese conmigo mediante el correo electrónico: pjriveramadera@yahoo.com

Muy respetuosamente,

Pablo Rivera Madera

I. INFORMACIÓN DEMOGRÁFICA:

1. País de Origen: _____
2. Denominación: _____
3. Grupo de Edad: (_20-25) (_26-35) (_36-50) (_51-64) (_65-Más)
4. Género: _Masculino   _Femenino
5. Educación: _Escuela Superior o menos Grado _Asociado BA MA DR
6. Área principal de estudio: _____
7. Es usted: _ministro ordenado/a   _Predicador/a Laico
_Tiempo ministerial
8. ¿Cuánto tiempo usted ha estado predicando en los E.U.?_____
_____
9. ¿Dónde desarrolla usted su ministerio de predicación en los E.U.?
_____
10. ¿Con que frecuencia predica a los hispanos/as? _____
_____
11. ¿En qué lenguaje usualmente predica? _____
12. ¿Cuál es su mayor objetivo al predicar a la comunidad hispana en E.U? _____

ENFOQUE DE LA PREDICACION PARA INMIGRANTES HISPANOS

¿Cuánto está usted de acuerdo o en desacuerdo con las siguientes aseveraciones sobre su predicación? (Marque una respuesta para cada aseveración)

	Completamente de Acuerdo	De Acuerdo	Desacuerdo	Completamente en Desacuerdo
1. Mi predicación a los hispanos/as combina teología, gestos, voz y retórica.				
2. Yo incluyo mis experiencias personales, puntos de vista y opiniones en el sermón.				

	Completamente de Acuerdo	De Acuerdo	Desacuerdo	Completamente en Desacuerdo
3. Yo selecciono el tema de mi sermón y uso el texto para sostenerlo.				
4. La situación y el contexto social dictan el propósito del sermón que yo predico.				
5. Yo preparo mi sermón tomando como base las necesidades y sacrificios de los hispanos/as en E.U.				
6. Yo menciono en mis sermones ilustraciones que hacen sentido a la cultura hispana.				
7. Yo coincido con los hispanos/as de que el sermón es Palabra de Dios.				
8. Yo predico por el leccionario.				
9. El sermón para la comunidad hispana debe estar enraizado en la Biblia.				
10. Yo escribo mis sermones y leo directamente del manuscrito.				

11. Durante el sermón hago preguntas a la congregación para conectarme con ellos y hacerlos partícipes.				
12. Yo incluyo chistes, anécdotas e ilustraciones como parte esencial del sermón en el contexto hispano.				
13. Los hispanos/as esperan un sermón profundo, ameno y directo.				
14. Los hispanos/as esperan un mensaje de esperanza y afirmación.				
15. Yo trato de evitar los textos que le recuerden a los hispanos/as sus experiencias de miedo y sufrimiento.				
16. Mi punto de partida para el sermón es la necesidad de los oyentes.				
17. Mis sermones se mueven de una verdad general a la experiencia particular.				
18. Mi sermón se mueve de la experiencia particular a la verdad general.				
19. El sermón que predico tiene introducción, varios puntos centrales y conclusión.				

	Completamente de Acuerdo	De Acuerdo	Desacuerdo	Completamente en Desacuerdo
20. Yo uso lenguaje popular de la calle y del mercado cuando predico a la comunidad hispana.				
21. Yo no escribo mis sermones pero preparo un bosquejo para predicar.				
22. Yo desarrollo mis ideas acerca del texto según desarrollo el sermón.				
23. Yo escribo mis sermones pero no los leo cuando predico a los hispanos/as.				
24. Yo sigo la lógica del texto bíblico sin proponer un tema o tesis para el sermón.				
25. Yo propongo un tema o tesis al estudiar el texto bíblico y la elaboro durante el sermón.				
26. Usualmente yo predico más de treinta minutos.				
27. Yo construyo mis sermones uniendo varios versos bíblicos, citando capítulos y versículos.				

28. Mi predicación es personal porque yo muestro mis emociones para conectar con la audiencia.				
29. A veces invito a la congregación a cantar antes, durante o después del sermón.				
30. Siempre oro con la congregación antes de exponer el sermón.				
31. A veces ilustro mis sermones con alguna dramatización del texto bíblico.				
32. Yo me alejo del pulpito y me acerco a las personas cuando predico.				
33. Los hispanos/as recitan alto y claro los versos que el predicador cita de la Biblia como señal de participación.				
34. El sermón y la Biblia tienen la misma autoridad en el contexto hispano.				
35. En mis sermones yo considero un pasaje bíblico pero uso un texto clave como guía.				
36. En mis sermones enfatizo la exegesis de los versos bíblicos de modo que reflejen el mensaje de la Biblia.				

	Completamente de Acuerdo	De Acuerdo	Desacuerdo	Completamente en Desacuerdo
37. En el contexto hispano yo tengo autoridad y libertad para exponer mis puntos de vista sobre el texto.				
38. El sermón es una actuación de la cual los hispanos/as esperan ser participes.				
39. El sermón para los hispanos/as incluye oración al principio y al final y la invitación al altar.				
40. Levantar las manos, la risa y el llanto son señales de efectividad del sermón.				
41. Los latinos/as estimulan al predicador/a a extender el tiempo del sermón cuando sienten que Dios les está hablando.				
42. Para los hispanos la respuesta a la invitación al altar mide la efectividad del sermón.				

Preguntas Generales:

¿Cuál es su mayor preocupación cuando predica en congregaciones de inmigrantes hispanos?

_____

_____

¿Cómo describe usted su modelo de predicación para la comunidad de inmigrantes hispanos?

_____

¿Cómo describe su estilo de predicación en el contexto hispano?

_____

¿Qué recomendaciones puede ofrecerle a predicadores/as no-hispanos que quieran alcanzar la comunidad de inmigrantes hispanos en los Estados Unidos?

_____

Selected Bibliography

Achtemeier, Elizabeth. *Creative Preaching.* Nashville: Abingdon, 1980.

Alan of Lille. *The Art of Preaching,* Cistercian Fathers Series, Number 23, trans. Gilian
R. Evans. Kalamazoo: Cistercian Publications, 1981.

Badillo, David A. *Latinos in the Immigrant Church.* Baltimore: The John Hopkins
University Press. 2006.

Baktis, Peter A. *Transition from Civilian Preaching to a Military Environment,*
Preaching, Vol. 17, No. 1, July-August 2001.

Bartow, Charles L. *God's Human Speech: A Practical Theology of Proclamation.* Grand
Rapids, Michigan: William B. Eerdmans Publishing Company, 1997.

Brooks, Gennifer Benjamin, *Preaching as a Liturgical Act,* Circuit Rider,
Januay/February, 2006.

Camarota, Steven A., 100 *Million More Projecting the Impact of Immigration on the U.S.*
Population, 2007 to 2060, Center for Immigration Studies *Backgrounder,* August
2007.

Chapel, Bryan. *Christ Centered Preaching: Redeeming the Expository Sermon*, 2d Ed. Grand Rapids, Michigan: Baker Academic, 2006.

Cooper, Donald R. and Pamela S. Schindler. *Business Research Methods: Culture*
Analysis. Eight edition. New York: McGraw Hill Higher Education, 2003.

Davis, Kenneth G. and Jorge L. Presmanes, *Preaching and Culture in Latino*
Congregations, Chicago: Training Publications, 2000.

De La Torre, Miguel A. and Edwin David Aponte. *Introducing Latino/a Theologies*.
Maryknoll, New Cork: Orbis Books, 2001.

De Vaus, David. *Surveys in Social Research* (3rd ed.), London: UCL Press, 1993.
Edwards, Paul. *The Practical Preacher: Handy Hints for Hesitant Homilist*. Collegeville,
Minnesota: The Liturgical Press, 1994.

Fant, Clyde E. *Bonhoeffer: Wordly Preaching*. Nashville: Thomas Nelson Inc.
Publishers, 1975.

Frankfort, Nachmias C. and Guerrero, A. Leon *Social Statistics for a Diverse Society.*
(3rd Ed.), Thousand Oaks, California: Pine Forge Press, 2002.

Fink, Arlene. *How to Conduct Surveys: A Step by Step Guide.*(3rd ed.), Thousand Oaks,
California: Sage Publications, Inc., 2006.

Gonzalez, Justo L. *Mañana: Christian Theology from a Hispanic Perspective*. Nashville:
Abingdon Press, 1990.

Gonzalez, Justo L. and Pablo A. Jimenez, *Pulpito: An Introduction for Hispanic*
Preaching (Nashville: Abingdon Press), 2005.

Graeme, Goldsworthy. *Preaching the Whole Bible as Christian Scripture: The*
Application of Biblical Theology to Expository Preaching. Grand Rapids, Michigan:
Eerdmans Publishing Co, 2000.

Guthrie, Glifton E. *From Pew to Pulpit: A Beginner's Guide to Preaching*, Nashville:
Abingdon Press, 2006.

Haddon Robinson. *Biblical Preaching*. Nashville: Abingdon, 1980.
—. *Biblical Preaching: The Development and Delivery of Expository Messages*, 2d Ed. Grand rapids, Michigan: Baker Academic, 2008.

Hamilton, Adam. *Unleashing the Word: Preaching With Relevance, Purpose and*
Passion. Nashville: Abingdon Press, 2003.

Heisler, Greg. *Spirit Led Preaching: The Holy Spirit's Role in Sermon Preparation and Delivery*, Nashville, Tennessee: B&H Publishing Group, 2007

Hernandez, Edwin I. et al., *Strengthening Hispanic Ministry across Denominations: A*
Call to Action by the Pulpit and Pew Research in Pastoral Leadership. Durham:
Duke Divinity School, 2005.

Howell, D.C. *Statistical Methods for Psychology*. 4th ed. Belmont, CA: Wadsworth
Publishing Company, 1997.

Hull, William H. *Strategic Preaching: The Role of the Pulpit in Pastoral Leadership*. St Louis, Missouri: Chalice Press, 2006.

Jabusch, Willard F. *The Person in the Pulpit: Preaching as Caring.* Nashville: Abingdon,
1981.

Jetter, Joseph R. Jr. *Crisis Preaching: Personal and Public.* Nashville: Abingdon,1998.

Johnson, Mark. *The Body in the Mind: The Bodily Basis of Meaning, Imagination and*
Reason. 1987.

Jones, Ilion T. *Principles and Practice of Preaching: A comprehensive Study of the Art of*
Sermon Construction. Nashville: Abingdon, 1981.

Keck, Leander E. *The Bible in the Pulpit.* Nashville: Abingdon, 1978.

Koller, Charles W. *How to Preach without Notes.* Grand Rapids, Michigan: Baker Books,
2008.

Lawton, Kim, *Immigration Fuels Hispanic Church Activity Latino Evangelicals have been Voting Republican, but may be Shifting,* Religion & Ethics News Weekly, 11
February 2006.

Lischer, Richard. *Theories of Preaching: Selected Readings in Homiletical Tradition.*
Durham, North Carolina: The Labyrinth Press, 1987.

—. *A Theology of Preaching: The Dynamics of the Gospel.* Revised Edition.
Eugene, Oregon: Wipf and Stock Publishers, 2001.

—. *The End of Words: The Language of Reconciliation in a Culture of Violence,*
Eugene, Oregon: Wipf and Stock Publishers, 2005.

Long Thomas G. The *Witness of Preaching*. Nashville: Abingdon, 1989.

Lowry, Eugene L. *The Sermon: Dancing the Edge of Mystery*. Nashville: Abingdon
Press. 1997.

Lundblad, Barbara K. *Transforming the Stone: Preaching through Resistance to Change.*
Nashville: Abingdon Press 2001.

Massey, James Earl. *Designing the Sermon: Order and Movement in Preaching*,
Nashville: Abingdon, 1981.

McClure, John S. *Best Advice for Preaching*. Minneapolis: Fortress Press, 1998.

Moore, K.A., *Time to take a Closer Look at Hispanic Children and Families*. Policy and
Public Human Services, 59, 8. nd.

Passel, Jeffrey S. The Size and Characteristics of the Unauthorized Migrant Population in the U.S. Estimates Based on the March 2005 Research Report Current Population
Survey, The Pew Hispanic Center, March 7, 2006.

Portes, Alejandro and Ruben G. Rumbaut. *A Portrait Immigrant America*. 3d ed.
Berkeley and Los Angeles: University of California Press, 2006.

Richard, Ramesh, *Preparing Evangelistic Sermons: A Seven Step Method for Preaching
Salvation*. Grand Rapids, Michigan: Baker Books, 2005

—. *Preparing Expository Sermons: A Seven Step Method for Biblical
Preaching*. Grand Rapids, Michigan: Baker Books, 2008

Rivera Madera, Pablo, *Proclamando en Tierra Extraña: Doce Sermones en Inglés para*

Predicadores Hispanos. Victoria, Canada: Trafford Publishing, 2008.

Rubin Allen and Earl A. Babin. *Research Methods for Social Work,* 5th
    ed., Belmont:
Thompson Learning, 2006.

Sanders, James A. *God has a Story Too: Sermons in Context*. Philadelphia:
    Fortress,
1980.

Scott, John R. W. *The Preacher's Portrait: Some New Testament Word
    Studies*. Grand
Rapids, Michigan: Wm. B. Eerdmans Publishing Company, 1977.

Shepherd, William A. *No Deed Greater than a Word: A New Approach
    to Biblical
Preaching*. Ohio: CSS Publishing Company. 1998.

Smith, Christine Marie. *Preaching Justice: Ethnic and Cultural
    Perspectives*. Cleveland,
Ohio: United Church Press, 1998.

Smith, Gregory A. *Report on Pew Forum and Public Life; U.S. Religion
    Survey*. Pew
Research Center for the People and Press, July 2006.

Stott, John R. W. *La Predicación: Puente entre Dos Mundos*. Grand
    Rapids, Michigan:
Libros Desafío, 2006.

Sue, Derald Wing and David Sue, *Counseling the Culturally Different,
    Theory and
Practice*. 2d ed. Canada: John Wiley and Sons, 1990

Thompson, Wm. D. *The Use of the Bible in Preaching*. Nashville:
    Abingdon. 1980.

Turabian Kate L. *A Manual for Writers of Term Papers, Theses, and Dissertations.* Sixth edition. Chicago and London: The University of Chicago Press, 1996.

United States Department of Commerce, Census Bureau (Washington, D.C.: U.S.
Government Printing Office), 2000.

Van Seters, Arthur. *Preaching As A Social Act: Theology and Practice.* Nashville:
Abingdon Press, 1988.

Ward, Richard. *Preaching as a Communicative Act: The Birth of a Performance"*
Reformed Liturgy and Music 30, no.2, 1996.

Willimon, William H. *Conversation with Barth on Preaching.* Nashville: Abingdon
Press, 2006.

Wilson, Paul Scott. Preaching and Its Partners: *Preaching and Homiletical Theory.* St.
Louise, Missouri: Chalice Press, 2004.